BECOMING LIKE
GOD
KABBALAH AND OUR ULTIMATE DESTINY

BECOMING LIKE
GOD

KABBALAH AND OUR ULTIMATE DESTINY

MICHAEL BERG

www.kabbalah.com™

For further information:

The Kabbalah Centre
155 E. 48th St., New York, NY 10017
1062 S. Robertson Blvd., Los Angeles, CA 90035

1.800.Kabbalah
www.kabbalah.com

First Edition
June 2004
Printed in USA
ISBN 1-57189-242-7

Design: Hyun Min Lee

May we all Become like God
revealing unconditional love
for humanity,
and together usher in the
new era of enlightenment and peace
for our children, and their children
and their children's children
and so on...

In love and appreciation for my children,
and all children everywhere.

ACKNOWLEDGMENTS

My parents, Rav and Karen Berg, have given me many gifts of incalculable value. However, the greatest gift they've given me (and millions of other people around the world) has been guidance in the 5,000-year-old spiritual wisdom known as Kabbalah. Since they began talking, writing, and teaching about Kabbalah, they have given its key concepts a degree of focus and clarity that has never been known before. Moreover, having conducted their own lives according to these spiritual principles, they have provided a living example of *Becoming Like God* in action. It is impossible for me to adequately express my gratitude to my parents, and I will never be able to repay them for what they have given me. Everything written here comes from what they've taught me, and I hope I've presented their teachings faithfully. With the deepest possible love and respect, I offer this book as a tribute to them.

I would also like to thank my brother Yehuda for being my friend and partner in the path of continuing our parents' dream to spread this wisdom to the entire world.

I would also like to thank Jai Collins, Paul Wolfe, Peter Guzzardi, and Esther Sibilia, who helped me put these ancient ideas onto paper with clarity.

My most important daily partner is my wife. There is so much I can say about Monica, but for me the most important is this: Without you I have nothing, with you I have everything.

TABLE OF CONTENTS

PROLOGUE:
AN OPEN LETTER

THIS BOOK IS A LETTER ADDRESSED TO THE INMATES OF A PRISON. IT'S A STRANGE PRISON, BECAUSE WITHIN ITS WALLS LIE MOUNTAINS AND RIVERS AND SUNSETS. IT CONTAINS RARE BIRDS AND RARE DIS-EASES, MINI-DRAMAS, MAXI-DRAMAS, MELO-DRAMAS, AND THE LATEST DVDS. THE PRISON HAS NO NAME, BUT OVER THE YEARS ITS INMATES CAME UP WITH ONE AND IT STUCK. THEY CALL IT LIFE. NO ONE GETS OUT FOR GOOD BEHAVIOR, AND IN THIS FACILITY EVERYONE IS SENTENCED TO DIE.

THAT'S WHY THIS LETTER IS ADDRESSED WITH GREAT PASSION AND URGENCY. YOU WHO READ IT, HOWEVER COMFORTABLE

YOUR SURROUNDINGS, ARE INHABITANTS OF
THIS PRISON, AS AM I. OUR PRISON'S HISTO-
RY IS LITTERED WITH LEGENDS OF ESCAPE
ATTEMPTS, AND RIFE WITH ADVICE FROM
ESCAPE EXPERTS, BUT PRISON LIFE HAS
PROCEEDED PRETTY MUCH UNCHANGED FOR
SEVERAL THOUSAND YEARS. WHICH IS TO
SAY THAT MOST PRISONERS AREN'T AWARE
THEY'RE IN PRISON.

BUT NOW AN INCREDIBLE OPPORTUNITY
HAS PRESENTED ITSELF. A HISTORICALLY
ORDAINED OPPORTUNITY. AN OPPORTUNITY
WRITTEN IN THE DNA CODE OF OUR UNI-
VERSE. A CRACK IN THE PRISON DOOR HAS
OPENED AND ALLOWED A SHAFT OF SUN-
LIGHT TO SHINE THROUGH.

CONSIDER THIS BOOK A REPORT FROM THAT
SUNLIGHT.

THAT SUNLIGHT EMANATES FROM THE
CREATOR OF OUR UNIVERSE. WE CAN FOL-
LOW IT TO ITS SOURCE, AND WHEN WE DO,
WE DISCOVER OUR OWN SOURCE. WHEN WE
DO, INSTEAD OF PRAYING TO GOD, OBEYING
GOD, FEARING GOD, OR REJECTING GOD, WE
BECOME LIKE GOD.

ON WHAT AUTHORITY DO I MAKE SUCH AN
EXTRAORDINARY STATEMENT? ON GOOD

AUTHORITY, NONE OF WHICH IS MINE. IN FACT, NOT A SINGLE TRUTH THAT I'M ABOUT TO REVEAL COMES FROM ME PERSONALLY. I'M MERELY A REPORTER, AND MY NEWS SOURCE IS A 5,000-YEAR-OLD BODY OF WISDOM CALLED KABBALAH. MY PRINCIPAL REFERENCE IS 23 VOLUMES OF ARAMAIC TEXT, WHICH COMPRISE THE CHIEF REPOSITORY OF KABBALAH'S WISDOM: THE ZOHAR. TWO THOUSAND YEARS AGO, THE ZOHAR REVEALED TRUTHS SCIENCE IS ONLY NOW CONFIRMING. I HAVE HAD THE UNUSUAL PRIVILEGE OF TRANSLATING THE ZOHAR— ITS FIRST COMPLETE ENGLISH TRANSLATION IN HISTORY AND A PROJECT THAT TOOK ME MORE THAN TEN YEARS.

IN HUMAN TERMS, MY AUTHORITY COMES FROM A LINEAGE OF GIANTS: KABBALISTS AND LUMINARIES WHO FOR THOUSANDS OF YEARS HAVE LIVED, REVEALED, AND TRANSMITTED THE TEACHINGS OF KABBALAH, SOMETIMES IN SECRET, SOMETIMES IN THE FACE OF GRAVE DANGER, BUT ALWAYS WITH THE CERTAINTY THAT A MOMENT IN TIME WOULD COME WHEN THIS KNOWLEDGE WOULD EMERGE FROM ITS PRIVATE, ESOTERIC REALM AND BE AVAILABLE TO EVERYONE ON EARTH. A MOMENT WHEN THE PRISON DOORS WOULD OPEN AND A LONG HISTORY OF PAIN, SUFFERING, AND DEATH

WOULD BE OVER. A MOMENT WHEN PEOPLE
WOULD BECOME LIKE GOD.

THAT MOMENT IS NOW.

— MICHAEL BERG

INTRODUCTION:

THE ROCK AND THE MOUNTAIN

A rock is hewn from a mountain. It has the same nature as the mountain, but when it is disconnected it is no longer called *mountain*, it is called *rock*. Not one atom of its essence has changed, yet pulling it from the mountain has made it something else. Put the rock back into the mountain and it's no longer a rock. So the rock's existence is determined not by its substance, but by its relation to the mountain that is its source.

Kabbalah teaches that just as rocks are hewn from mountains, humans emerge from God. **AT THE LEVEL OF THE SOUL, HUMANS HAVE EXACTLY THE SAME ESSENCE AS GOD. IN ESSENCE HUMANS ARE LIKE GOD.**

SO, HOW DID WE BECOME ROCKS?

Kabbalah speaks of a negative force in the universe, a pickaxe that removes us from God. This force bears an odd name, but you will be quite familiar with it by the end of this book. **IT IS CALLED *DESIRE TO RECEIVE FOR THE SELF ALONE.* IT IS ALSO KNOWN AS EGO NATURE, A STATE VIRTUALLY ALL OF US INHABIT VIRTUALLY ALL OF THE TIME. AND IT IS THE SOURCE OF ALL OUR PAIN AND SUFFERING.**

So here's what this book is about: overcoming that force; revealing our true essence; becoming like God.

This book is a guide to that ultimate journey. It is meant to point the way; to motivate; to offer tools, direction, and encouragement. I offer it on behalf of the luminaries who have preceded me, sages who completed their own journeys to becoming like God and left behind a road map for the rest of us. The list of mapmakers begins with Abraham and Moses and spans centuries to include Kabbalists such as Rav Shimon bar Yochai, Rav Isaac Luria, and the Baal Shem Tov. Most notably, in the last century, Rav Ashlag received divine authorization to reveal information from Kabbalah that

DESIRE TO RECEIVE
FOR THE SELF ALONE

ROCK (YOU)   MOUNTAIN (GOD)

had been held secret for time immemorial. He was the first Kabbalist to write down wisdom that for thousands of years had only been transmitted orally from teacher to student.

So you might say this book is made possible by a grant from the universe. Thanks to that divine decision, and to the window in the cosmos that has opened in this era, the wisdom of Kabbalah now can be made available to every man, woman, and child.

A note before we go further: The word *God* is not an ideal term. No word has ever borne such a burden of interpretation and misinterpretation. For this reason, Kabbalists rarely use the word. *Light of the Creator* is a more accurate expression, because the Creator we know is an energy of sharing and fulfillment. It is the Light of the Creator we experience in those moments when joy overtakes us, or when beauty suddenly illuminates our lives.

Having said that, since the word *God* is widely understood to represent a divine being of total perfection and ultimate potential, we will use it here in that sense, neutral of any set of religious beliefs.

Once, a group of souls descended to this world on a long ladder. Reaching the bottom rung, they sighed, dropped into the world, and became human beings. They sighed, knowing that their birth into this world meant separating from God.

As their days on Earth went by, they repeatedly jumped into the air to grab the bottom rung of the ladder, in a vain attempt to climb back to heaven. Some jumped a few times, then gave up and settled into human existence. Others jumped hundreds, even thousands of times, but they too failed to reach the ladder.

One person, however, was different. He began jumping, kept jumping, then, unlike the others, never stopped jumping. Finally, God picked him up and brought him back to heaven.

It may not look like it, but this book is a big neon sign. Its message is **KEEP JUMPING. THE TASK IS UNCEASING. KEEP JUMPING. THE WORRIES OF LIFE MAY SEEM INSURMOUNTABLE. KEEP JUMPING. WE MAY EVEN FORGET WHAT WE'RE TRYING TO REACH. KEEP JUMPING.**

And if we have a question, it is not to ask why or when or who or what.

THE ONLY QUESTION IS: AM I LIKE GOD YET?

DESIRE TO RECEIVE
FOR THE SELF ALONE

ROCK (YOU)   MOUNTAIN (GOD)

CHAPTER ONE:

A CRACK IN THE PRISON DOOR

There once was a prince who lived in a grand palace. It was filled with treasures from every corner of the earth: Persian rugs, French tapestries, hand-carved tables, and the finest paintings from Europe and Asia. Its rooms overflowed with silver platters of fruit, orchids, and bouquets of exotic flowers.

But there was a problem: Shutters were fastened across every window. Not a single ray of sunlight penetrated, and the palace lay in darkness. The problem was that the prince was oblivious to the abundance surrounding him.

One day, a servant plucked up the courage to ask the prince why he inhabited a palace as dark as the blackest night, and the prince was stunned. He had no idea there was an alternative. Joyfully, the servant opened the palace shutters for the first time, and suddenly the prince could see beauty and abundance everywhere. They had been within reach all along. He simply had been unable to see them.

Like the shutters in this story, there is a crack in our prison door.

We don't know how it got there. But it changes everything.

Sunlight floods the darkness and images of an immensely joyful world dance on the walls.
SUDDENLY, WE REALIZE THE PRISON IS NOT REALLY THE WORLD, AS WE'VE BEEN LED TO BELIEVE. IT IS MERELY A PRISON. A PRISON WITH HIGH-SPEED INTERNET ACCESS, PERHAPS, BUT A PRISON NEVERTHELESS, WHOSE WALLS ARE SUFFERING AND WHOSE GATES ARE DEATH.

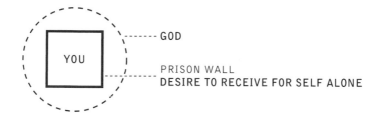

The crack in the door challenges us to a merciless assessment of our situation, the R-rated version, not the PG version. **WE MUST REALIZE THAT THIS LIFE IS A PRISON.** Rather than generating despair, such an evaluation is actually an assertion of freedom and hope. **VANISHING IN TIME, DESTINED TO DIE, CLINGING TO AN ILLUSION OF SEPARATENESS FROM GOD—THESE ARE THE ULTIMATE SOURCES OF DESPERATION. REPLACING THEM REQUIRES A DECISION. CROSSING A LINE.** It's as if we were in a destructive, unhealthy situation, a demeaning love relationship or an unfulfilling job, and after all the denials and rationalizations, we're struck by a moment of clarity and it suddenly pops. There's no more balance sheet, no more judicious weighing of the various pros and cons. We just leave, because we know we have to.

That is the fierceness of commitment necessary to vacate this existence of pain and suffering and return to a world of joy. **THE JOURNEY TO BECOMING LIKE GOD MUST BECOME MORE THAN AN INTRIGUING IDEA. IT MUST BECOME A REALIZATION THAT ENTERS OUR CELLS WITH THE**

FORCE OF DESTINY, a realization that seamless union with God—where God's thoughts become our thoughts, God's actions our actions, God's intentions our intentions—is a natural process, not a religious conversion. It is a transformation taking place in an invisible place in our souls, as natural as a seed becoming an oak tree, and it has nothing to do with faith, morality, or earning heaven on the basis of good behavior. It is a transformation born of the most ancient science of truth of all, Kabbalah, and Kabbalah is not religion but rather technology—technology that predates religion.

The question becomes why, if escape is such a natural process, is it a road so untraveled? Why have so few in history succeeded in breaking free of these prison walls? The answer is that the **PATH OF ESCAPE LEADS PAST THE ULTIMATE PRISON GUARD, THE NEGATIVE FORCE ANCIENT TEXTS REFER TO AS *DESIRE TO RECEIVE FOR THE SELF ALONE*. IT IS A FORCE PROGRAMMED INTO THE ATOMS OF PHYSICAL NATURE THAT OPPOSES EVERY EFFORT WE MAKE TO CHANGE.** So from this moment on, I will give this force a name: *The Opponent.*

Unless we understand the insidious nature of the Opponent, there is no hope of escape. The Opponent comes dressed in the clothes of a friend, rather than the uniform of a guard, and then betrays us endlessly to our captors. Even worse, **THE OPPONENT CON-**

VINCES US THAT *HE IS US*. WHAT WE CALL LIFE IS A VAST CASE OF MISTAKEN IDENTITY, AND UNTIL WE DISTINGUISH OUR IDENTITY FROM THE OPPONENT'S, WE WILL REMAIN IMPRISONED.

So, let's begin a journey on a highway of transformation, driven by revulsion for the Opponent. A journey conducted endlessly, relentlessly, and joyfully, asking ourselves at each moment, Is this choice moving me closer or further from God?

Of course, the mind will say, *This is just a book. It can't be serious. What chance do I have of remembering this godly nature I supposedly possess every time I make a decision? How could I scale walls so few before me have ever scaled?*

The Opponent is pleased you feel that way.

But the Wright brothers didn't feel that way. Nor did Leonardo da Vinci. **AT EACH SHIFT OF THE PARADIGM, THE *IMPOSSIBLE* PRESENTS ITS IMPECCABLE CREDENTIALS, IS OVERRULED, AND THE UNTHINKABLE BECOMES THE NORM.**

And now another seismic shift has occurred. We have the fortune to be alive for the most extraordinary moment in the history of human consciousness. It is a time when what was once absurd will become commonplace: **IT IS NOW POSSIBLE FOR LARGE NUMBERS OF PEOPLE TO ESCAPE THE PRISON OF PAIN, SUFFERING, AND DEATH. AND BY DOING SO, THEY'LL FORM A CRITICAL MASS THAT WILL CHANGE THE WORLD FOR EVERYONE ELSE.**

Now it's just a matter of mechanics. With what tiny blunt instrument will we chip away at the walls of the dungeon, day after day, year after, until the day we breathe in sunlight?

We'll get there.

What hope do we have against the insidious, shape-shifting guard who stands at the prison's gates?

We'll get there.

This book is an invitation to a journey, the supreme journey, from prisoner to God. It is extended to you courtesy of a crack in the door that has just opened up in this era in which we happen to be fortunate enough to live.

CHAPTER TWO:

GOD DISGUISED
AS YOU

The guard at the prison gate is utterly ruthless. Brutal treatment of prisoners has proceeded for millennia, so now the prisoners are beaten, hopeless, huddling on their cots, staring out through the bars of their cells. A good day is simply one endured without pain.

The guard, the Opponent, has convinced his prisoners that we're small and insignificant, when in truth, whatever our wildest dreams of accomplishment may be, they only scratch the surface of what is possible.

THE TRUTH IS, WE ARE DESTINED TO BECOME LIKE GOD BUT HAVE BEEN TRICKED INTO BECOMING INMATES, POSING AS ANTS, INDIFFERENT TO THE GHASTLY SPREAD BETWEEN WHAT WE ARE AND WHAT WE COULD BE. We bounce back and forth between actions and reactions. We could be infinite. And until we begin to realize that potential, we will lie listless on our prison cots.

According to the Bible, "Man was created in God's image, in God's image man was created." Kabbalah teaches that there are no superfluous words in the Bible, so why the repetition? It urges the reader to pay attention. **DO NOT MISS THIS. YOU ARE CREATED IN GOD'S IMAGE.**

YOU HAVE THE SAME ESSENCE AND THEREFORE THE SAME POTENTIAL AS GOD. YOU ARE DESTINED TO BECOME LIKE GOD, SO KEEP ASKING YOURSELF, AM I LIKE GOD YET? AM I MANIFESTING GODLY POWERS? CAN I HEAL THE SICK AND BLESS PEOPLE? HAVE I RESURRECTED THE DEAD? THE YARDSTICK SUDDENLY EXTENDS TO INFINITY. I DON'T JUST MEASURE MYSELF AGAINST MYSELF. I MEASURE MYSELF AGAINST GOD.

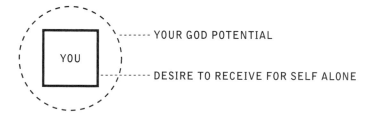

This is our potential, whoever we are, whatever our impediments, real or imagined. Moses was physically

frail and spoke with a lisp. Greatness is not reserved for the great. **THE GREAT ARE SIMPLY THOSE WHO HAVE RISEN TO MEET THEIR DESTINY.** Everyone alive has a destiny infinitely richer than they know.

Dullness and boredom come from unmet or abandoned potential. It's television ratings soaring. It's playing computer games when you were meant to compose sonatas. **IF YOU'RE NOT DOING WHAT YOU WERE MEANT TO DO—AND EACH PERSON WAS MEANT FOR SOMETHING ASTONISH-ING—YOU'LL NEVER ENJOY CONTENTMENT.** Imagine Dr. Jonas Salk becoming a successful businessman, a generous citizen, and a wonderful father, but never going near a lab. What may have seemed a good life would in fact have been tragic, the pain and suffering he was meant to remove from the world never having been achieved.

A great spiritual leader with thousands of students and many books to his credit once told his story.

> *When I was eleven, he said, I was a lost cause as a student. I never minded my teachers and I played hooky from school at every opportunity. Then one evening, I heard my parents in the next room talking about me. My mother was crying.*
>
> *"What are we going to do with our son?"*

she said to my father. "He has no interest in his studies. He doesn't want go to school, and any day now they will expel him. Then what will become of him?"

As I listened to her, a strange event occurred: I could feel her anguish as acutely as if it had been my own. I burst into the room and I told her I was sorry. I promised that I would be a good student and obedient from that moment on. I made the promise not because I cared about studying but because I cared about my mother and did not want to cause her pain. I kept my word and changed my ways. I became studious and never missed a day of school, and I grew up to be the scholar you see before you now.

My point is this: If I had not overheard my parents that day, what would have become of me? Well, I would have been a good person, since it was in my nature to do so. I would have prayed, I would have given to charity, I would have enabled many others to earn a good living. However, imagine what would have happened after I left this world and arrived in the place called the "heavenly court."

My judges would say, "Where are your thousands of students?"

YOUR GOD POTENTIAL

YOU

DESIRE TO RECEIVE FOR SELF ALONE

I would gape at them and reply, "What are you talking about? I was a merchant and I did good business, but I didn't have any information to impart to even a handful of students, let alone thousands. Let's talk instead about the sums of money I gave to charity."

And then they would say, "Where are the dozens of books you were supposed to write?"

Again, I'd look at them as if they were unhinged. "What do you mean, 'dozens of books?' I wasn't illiterate—I could read and write—but I had no reason to write any books; I had nothing to teach anyone. Let's talk instead about the many kindnesses I bestowed on my friends, my family, and my customers."

Then they would show me everything I could have achieved, everything I should have done. Can you imagine the grief I would feel in that moment? There is no greater hell than to see what we might have done, but in fact failed to do.

SO THIS IS THE MEASURE: WHERE AM I, NOT IN REFERENCE TO OTHERS, BUT IN REFER-

ENCE TO MYSELF? WHERE AM I ON THE ROAD OF MY OWN POTENTIAL? Growth should not be linear, but exponential. A little growth increases our feeling of contentment exponentially and every step makes the next one easier.

If our thoughts and actions are not taking us toward God, we need to change. What progress are we making? That cannot be quantified by anyone outside ourselves. **WE NEED TO ASK OURSELVES THIS: IF WE CONTINUE IN OUR LIFE'S TRAJECTORY FOR 5, 10, OR 20 YEARS, WHERE WILL WE BE? WILL WE BECOME LIKE GOD YET?** The answer should make us rethink our efforts. As we dissolve our prison chains and merge our essence back into God's essence, we reveal our godly nature more and more. Eventually, we may become immortal, and even resurrect the dead. It is this vision we keep before us, immovably.

Until then, the Opponent will do his job as supreme prison guard of the penitentiary we inhabit, and chief operating officer of our universal system of pain and suffering. His job is to ensure that we don't realize our potential, yet if we could even believe for a minute who we really were and how great our destiny, the balance would shift and we would emerge from prison, not like inmates, but like God.

YOUR GOD POTENTIAL

YOU

DESIRE TO RECEIVE FOR SELF ALONE

THE WORLD IN THE BALANCE

We are trapped in a paradigm of insignificance. What we say doesn't matter. What we do has no effect. We are isolated, separate, finite. We are rocks.

REALIZING OUR POTENTIAL SHATTERS THE PARADIGM OF INSIGNIFICANCE AND LEADS TO A FURTHER REALIZATION: EVERYTHING MATTERS; EVERYTHING COUNTS; EVERY-THING AFFECTS EVERYTHING ELSE.

THE OPPONENT HAS US CONVINCED OF OUR POWERLESSNESS, WHEN WITH EVERY ACTION, THE WORLD STANDS IN THE BAL-ANCE AND WE ARE TIPPING THE SCALES. If we commit a negative action today, someone halfway around the world may receive the negative energy our action released into the universe. In turn, he will be tipped toward doing something negative and the nega-tivity will grow exponentially. Ultimately, it will come back to the person who originated it.

In the time of the great Kabbalist Rav Isaac Luria, there lived an eminent sage and scholar named Rav Yosef Karo. Once, after weeks of meditation on a difficult passage of the Bible, Rav Karo penetrated its deepest meaning. Delighted, he posed the question to a student, expecting the student would appreciate his master's explanation. To his surprise, the student immediately saw the answer. Rav Karo could not believe that what had taken him weeks of intense study to uncover had taken the student a few minutes.

Despondent, he began questioning himself. Perhaps he had been given too much credit. Perhaps he should give up teaching. He wandered the streets and encountered the eminent Rav Luria, who asked him why he looked so downcast. After listening patiently, Luria spoke.

"There was a village whose water came from a spring at the top of a mountain. Few villagers had the strength to walk to the top, so it was one man's job to fetch water for the entire village. It took him many hours to fill the huge buckets. When he did, everyone came and filled their little cups from these buckets, which of course took only minutes. Even the weakest of them had no trouble.

"What I'm saying is that your weeks of work opened up a channel of understanding. Once the channel was open, it was simple for your student to also understand."

YOUR GOD POTENTIAL

YOU

DESIRE TO RECEIVE FOR SELF ALONE

What we think and what we do enters the global consciousness and changes it. According to Rav Ashlag, every time a person removes even a fragment of the Desire to Receive for the Self Alone, the increase in consciousness accrues to the global soul. Each time one of us reveals more of his or her godly nature, it influences the collective Being.

AS YOU BECOME LIKE GOD, IT BECOMES EASIER FOR SOMEONE ELSE TO BECOME LIKE GOD. THE WORLD HANGS IN THE BALANCE.

CHAPTER THREE:

CERTAINTY

*During the nine months we spend in our
mother's womb, an angel holds a candle for
us, teaching us the wisdom of the universe.
We behold everything, from the beginning of
the world to the end of the world. When we
are born, the angel gives us a sharp blow on
the upper lip and it makes us forget everything we have learned. Yet memory traces
remain in our souls, the idea of God resonates with us, and it is on this resonance,
on these residual memories, that we build
our consciousness.*

– kabbalistic tale

We enter the physical world, our selves forgotten.

But somewhere in our souls we remember something. The potential to become like God stirs.

These memories are the basis for what Kabbalists call *certainty*. Certainty, according to the Zohar, is one of the secrets to activating our godly nature—certainty not only that we *can* achieve it, but that we *will* achieve it.

Certainty is a vessel.

According to Kabbalah, **IN ORDER FOR THE LIGHT OF THE CREATOR TO BE REVEALED, THERE MUST BE A VESSEL TO RECEIVE IT. THE NAME OF THAT VESSEL IS CERTAINTY, AND THE LEVEL OF LIGHT REVEALED DEPENDS ON THE STRENGTH OF THAT CERTAINTY.** The Zohar states that there is never a time when there is no Light. It is only the vessel that limits the amount of Light manifested. When we achieve total certainty, we become like God.

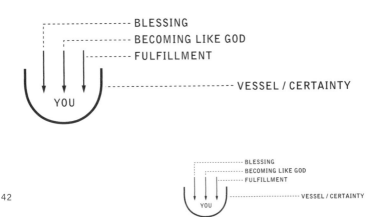

The Opponent is anti-certainty. **THE OPPONENT IS THE SOWER OF DOUBT, THE RESTRICTOR OF THE VESSEL. IN THE OPPONENT'S PARADIGM OF INSIGNIFICANCE, WE DON'T BECOME LIKE GOD BECAUSE WE BELIEVE WE CAN'T BECOME LIKE GOD.**

The Bible tells the story of a woman from Shunam, who cared for Elisha the Prophet.

"You've taken such good care of me," Elisha told the woman one day. "What shall I do for you? Can I intercede with the king on some matter, or with one of his generals? How might I be of service to you?"

The Shunamit replied that she was a simple woman with no special requests. But after she had left, Elisha asked aloud, "What can I do for this loyal woman?"

Gehazi, his servant, answered, "Master, the Shunamit is an old woman and she has never had a child."

Elisha called her back and said to her, "You will give birth to a son," specifying the exact day the boy would be born. Astounded, the Shunamit answered, "Do not mock me. Do not lie to me," but Elisha reassured her calmly that it would come to pass exactly as prophesied. And it did. She gave birth to a baby boy on the precise day of Elisha's prophecy.

Years passed and the child grew. One day, while cutting hay in the fields, the boy complained of a headache. His condition worsened, and later, while sitting on his mother's lap, he died.

The Shunamit carried the boy to the bed where Elisha would sleep when he was in town, and laid him on it. She closed the door behind her, went to her husband, and said, "Send me one of the servants—one of the young ones who work with you—and also one of the donkeys, and let me go to the Man of God, who is teaching on the edge of town." The husband inquired why she was going to the prophet, since it was neither the first of the month nor the Sabbath, but the Shunamit said simply, "Peace be with you. Good-bye."

She rode to Mount Carmel where Elisha was teaching, and when the prophet saw her, he asked Gehazi to inquire about her family. The Shunamit told the servant that everything was fine. However, when she reached the place where Elisha stood, she

BLESSING
BECOMING LIKE GOD
FULFILLMENT

VESSEL / CERTAINTY

YOU

clasped her hands around his legs. Gehazi came to push her away, but the prophet said, "Leave her. She is in great pain. God did not let me know this; He did not let me see, and He did not tell me."

Through her tears, the woman cried, "Did I ask for a son from God? I did not. I begged you not to make a fool of me. What kind of favor was it to give me a son who dies at such a young age?"

Elisha told Gehazi to put on a cloak, take Elisha's cane, and go and place it on the child's face. "If you come across anyone," Elisha warned him, "do not talk about this. Even if someone blesses you, don't answer them."

The woman stuck close to Gehazi as he headed toward the child, swearing she would not leave his side until he had revived her son. However, in spite of Elisha's warning and the Shunamit's protestations, Gehazi mentioned his mission to several acquaintances he encountered. When they reached the child, he put the cane on the boy's face, as Elisha had instructed, but nothing happened. The boy was as still as a rock, without even the flicker of an eyelid. Gehazi and the Shunamit rushed back to

Elisha, and the mother began to sob uncontrollably. Elisha put on his coat and made the journey himself back to the house.

Elisha closed the bedroom door behind him, prayed to God, and then lay down on top of the child. He put his mouth on the boy's mouth, his eyes on the boy's eyes, and his hands on the boy's hands. Slowly, the body of the child became warm. Elisha got up, paced around the room for a few moments, and then lay down again on the boy. He repeated this procedure seven times, and after the seventh time the child opened his eyes. The prophet told Gehazi to call in the Shunamit. She entered the room and, upon seeing her son alive, she fell to her knees and bowed down to Elisha. Weeping, but now with tears of joy, she lifted up her child and departed.

This is the story of the vessel known as certainty, encrypted with many levels of coded meaning.

Why does the woman say good-bye to her husband rather than inform him of the son's death?

The answer resides in the technology of certainty. **WHEN WE DON'T BELIEVE DEATH CAN BE OVERCOME, IT WILL NOT HAPPEN. LACK OF CERTAINTY CLOSES OFF THE VESSEL.** The

Shunamit did not confide in her husband because she knew his level of certainty could not encompass their son returning from the dead. Had she told her husband, the prophet would have been unable to perform the miracle. The father would certainly have prayed for his son's resurrection. He would have dearly loved to believe in its possibility. But wanting to believe is not the same as certainty. Good intentions still limit the vessel.

Such is the insidious power of doubt. Many consider the Bible the word of God, yet refuse to believe in the possibility of resurrection, even though it is declared in the Bible's pages. This is the Opponent at work, sowing his seeds in the fields of pain, suffering, and death, convincing us we can't become like God. For the Opponent knows the power of certainty awakened, the ultimate knowing of who we are and what we can become like: God.

With certainty as a foundation we can approach what follows: an extraordinary set of statements that will change our lives forever.

CHAPTER FOUR:
THE GOD
FORMULA

So, we inhabit a prison—a strange sort of prison, to be sure, because most inmates don't even realize we're behind bars. We're even conditioned to scoff at the notion that there might actually be another world, a world of joy and Light, shining right beyond the prison walls.

Then, one day, someone hands us an escape plan that includes a layout of the prison and a step-by-step plan of escape. A flawless plan.

What will we do?

What I'm about to reveal is a blueprint to freedom. Of course, we don't literally live inside prison walls, and we're not literally confined to dingy concrete cells, but we are trapped by pain, suffering, and death. **SO, IN FACT, WHAT I'M ABOUT TO PRESENT IS AN ESCAPE PLAN FROM THE STRONGEST MAXIMUM-SECURITY PRISON EVER BUILT.**

If that's true, if, unlike Club Med, life is *not* as it should be, if there really is a life of joy and abundance destined for us by the Creator, **LOGIC WOULD DICTATE THAT THE PLAN I'M ABOUT TO REVEAL IS MORE THAN AN INTERESTING PIECE OF ADVICE. IT'S MORE THAN ANOTHER BOOK OF POSITIVE INFORMATION ABOUT LIFE TO READ AND FORGET. IF THIS TRULY IS A VIABLE ESCAPE PLAN, LOGIC DICTATES THAT THIS IS THE MOST IMPORTANT PIECE OF INFORMATION THAT HAS EVER COME YOUR WAY. IT SHOULD NOT JUST BE READ, IT SHOULD BE SEIZED. IT SHOULD BE STUDIED AND MEMORIZED, OR COPIED AND PUT IN YOUR POCKET SO YOU CAN READ IT ON THE STREET, OR TAPED TO THE MIRROR SO IT'S THE FIRST THING YOU SEE WHEN YOU WAKE UP.**

This plan involves six statements and what I call the God Formula. The six statements that follow serve as an explanation of life as it is, and life as it should be. The God Formula provides a method for getting from one to the other. It is rigorously logical, yet it is not a product of human reason. It is born of information revealed over millennia to men whose fate it has been to receive such truths and relay them to the rest of us.

It is a message from the other side of the wall, a shaft of sunlight pouring through a crack in the prison door.

1. THE WORLD IS THE WAR OF TWO OPPOSITE FORCES: LIGHT AND DARKNESS.

There is no permanence in the universe. There is only movement. We are either heading toward the Light or we're heading for Darkness. Through our actions, we choose our direction.

2. THE SOURCE OF LIGHT, BETTER KNOWN AS GOD, IS THE WELLSPRING OF ALL JOY, FULFILLMENT, AND LIFE. THE FORCE OF DARKNESS, BETTER KNOWN AS EGO NATURE, IS THE SOURCE OF ALL PAIN, SUFFERING, AND DEATH.

All the positive things we experience in our lives are manifestations of the Light of the Creator. Ego is the state of total disconnection from God's Light; therefore, it brings complete Darkness. We navigate between these two forces. When we are in the clutches of the Desire to Receive for the Self Alone, we veer ever closer to Darkness. There we feast on a steady diet of chaos and sickness and are finally sentenced to death.

3. WE CREATE OUR LIVES BY WHICHEVER FORCE WE CONNECT TO.

There is a choice to be made at every moment.

We have the power to choose our reality. Each moment, we can connect in varying degrees to Light and to Darkness, depending on our actions. To the degree our actions connect to God, we will experience Light and fulfillment. To the degree our actions connect to Darkness and ego, we will experience pain.

As we choose to move closer to the Light, we will experience a greater degree of fulfillment and less pain.

As we choose to move closer to ego nature and the absence of God's Light, we increase our experience of pain and decrease our fulfillment.

Those are our only choices.

4. WE CONNECT TO THE TWO FORCES THROUGH THE LAW OF SIMILARITY OF FORM: WE CONNECT TO AND BECOME WHAT WE BECOME *LIKE*.

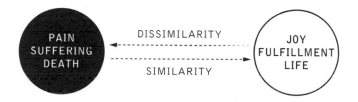

We're accustomed to the idea of things being separated by space.

On a deeper level, things are separated or connected by a similarity or dissimilarity of form. We're separated from God, for example, because we're not like Him; we don't match His essence. His is an essence of sharing, and ours is of receiving.

According to the Law of Similarity of Form, when essences match, the separation ends. This means that as our essence becomes more like God's essence, we move closer to being like God.

Another way to say this is, we become like God by behaving *like* God.

5. WE BECOME LIKE GOD BY SYSTEMATICALLY DESTROYING THE EGO, BECAUSE THE DESIRE TO RECEIVE FOR THE SELF ALONE IS THE OPPOSITE OF GOD. HE DOES NOT RECEIVE FROM ANYONE.

Through a cosmic case of mistaken identity, we connect to the ego, to a dissimilarity of nature with God. The world has been carefully designed by the Opponent for the care and feeding of that ego—the endless craving for respect, vanity, praise, and flattery, and the ceaseless indulgence of selfish desires.

To achieve similarity of form, to match God's essence, we must move wholeheartedly in the opposite direction: to confronting, humiliating, embarrassing, and purging that ego nature rather than propping it up, and freeing ourselves from the need to indulge selfish desires, until our essence finally becomes like God's essence.

6. WE BECOME LIKE GOD BY TRANSFORMING INTO BEINGS OF SHARING, BECAUSE GOD IS A FORCE OF INFINITE SHARING.

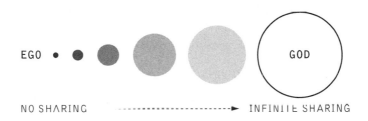

EGO •

NO SHARING · ➤ INFINITE SHARING

GOD

Desire to Receive for the Self Alone is the opposite of God's nature, which is a nature of infinite sharing. By opposing this selfish desire and becoming beings of sharing, we match God's essence. Transforming into a being of sharing does not mean performing an occasional act of generosity. It mandates continual movement toward the Light and a change of form: to become a being in which every thought, every action, and every utterance comes from the Desire to Share.

This transformation, in which sharing becomes a way of living, not merely an occasional act, in which sharing is done when it is not easy or comfortable to share, bears a special name.

It is called transformative sharing.

THE GOD FORMULA

THROUGH A DUAL PROCESS OF ERADICATING THE EGO AND PERFORMING TRANSFORMATIVE SHARING, WE AWAKEN OUR TRUE NATURE AND BECOME LIKE GOD, CREATING A LIFE OF TOTAL JOY AND FULFILLMENT.

Wherever we can, we must take actions to destroy the ego. Conversely, we won't dread embarrassing and humiliating situations anymore; we will welcome them, because they help us destroy the ego and realize our true nature.

Wherever we can, we share, especially when it's not easy or comfortable to do so.

When we live as God, we realize God's nature in every cell and we eradicate the barriers between our true nature and ourselves.

When we do not live like God, we live in separation, in ego nature, in the Desire to Receive for the Self Alone. Here, each desire makes our separation more solid, sentencing us to pain, suffering, and death.

So, we have a job to do in this physical realm: continually rooting out the Desire to Receive for the Self Alone. Moment to moment, in every moment of now, we must operate as beings of sharing.

Our job is to become like God.

CHAPTER FIVE

YOUR LIFE CHANGES NOW

Now we know the formula.

We're either heading toward life or we're heading toward death. Step by step, we'll either achieve complete and utter connection with God—and pain, suffering, and death will disappear from this world—or we'll achieve complete disconnection from God and we'll die. **RIGHT NOW, THIS MINUTE, AS YOU READ THESE WORDS, YOU'RE EITHER HEADING FOR ETERNAL LIFE OR YOU'RE COMMITTING SUICIDE.**

This realization is not a paradigm shift. It's a paradigm shattering. And yet, given that you have found this book among millions of others and have accompanied me so far, chances are you know this is true.

GOD EXISTS. AND HE WOULD NEVER CON-SIGN THE HUMAN RACE TO ENDLESS SUF-FERING AND UNAVOIDABLE DEATH. UNION WITH GOD IS POSSIBLE, AND ITS CONSE-QUENCE IS NEVER-ENDING JOY AND THE REMOVAL OF DEATH. GOD DOES NOT SUFFER AND DIE; THEREFORE, WE DON'T NEED TO SUFFER AND DIE.

So, the only question is where to begin.

WE BEGIN WITH RUTHLESS HONESTY ABOUT OUR PRESENT STATE. We must name the extent to which selfishness governs our every action. We must focus the truth upon ourselves and reveal that everything we do is born of selfish desire. The Desire to Receive for the Self Alone is in perma-nent ON position. This is most true when we think we're acting selflessly. When we make a donation, help our neighbor, go the extra mile at work, pray for humanity in a place of prayer, what are we actually doing? We're trying to gain advantage for ourselves, or our agenda may be to feel good about ourselves. It may be to appear spiritual in the eyes of the world. But a pure gaze on our motives suggests our motives are rarely pure.

THE GOD FORMULA IS A TWO-TIERED ASSAULT ON THE EGO: THE PROCESS OF DESTROYING OUR EGO ON THE INSIDE AND

PERFORMING TRANSFORMATIVE SHARING ON THE OUTSIDE. AN ASSAULT WITH NO REST, NO COMPROMISE, AND ONE CONSTANT LITMUS TEST: AM I GOD YET OR AM I NOT?

The process of destroying ego is not a moral decision. It's a down-to-earth, hardheaded, practical decision, because it leads to happiness and fulfillment.

Transformative sharing does not come automatically; rather, it violates our sense of entitlement. It is so contrary to our nature, in fact, that it changes our nature itself. Sharing and ego are inversely proportional, just as a wall and sunlight are inversely proportional: The more wall, the less sun. The less wall, the more sun. **WE SHARE WITH OTHERS SO WE CAN TRULY GIVE TO OURSELVES.**

TRUE SELFISHNESS

Kabbalists teach that the world was created with a single purpose: to provide the Creator with an opportunity to share His abundance with His creations. With that purpose in mind, the Creator shaped vessels to receive that abundance. These vessels sometimes bear the name "human beings."

Unfortunately, we vessels have underperformed in our promise.

WE WERE DESIGNED TO BECOME ONE WITH OUR CREATOR. WE WERE BUILT TO HOLD AN INFINITE PAYLOAD OF HEALTH, JOY, AND LIFE. INSTEAD, WE CONTAIN A LITTLE HEALTH, A FEW INFINITESIMAL DROPS OF JOY, AND ABOUT 75 YEARS OF PAIN AND SUFFERING. Instead of being infinite, we're like thimbles in a vast ocean of life. What happened?

We vessels, it turns out, were constructed with a defective material called Desire to Receive for the Self Alone. **WHEN THE SELF IS PREOCCUPIED WITH ITS OWN DESIRES, OBSESSED WITH ITS OWN SURVIVAL, AND DRIVEN BY HUNGER FOR IMMEDIATE GRATIFICATION, THE SELF BECOMES OPAQUE TO THE CREATOR'S LIGHT. WE VESSELS FAIL, NOT BECAUSE WE WANT TO RECEIVE, BUT BECAUSE WE WANT TO RECEIVE SO LITTLE.** As the great Kabbalist Rav Ashlag said, there's nothing wrong with desire itself. It's just that the vessel we use to receive our desire is so limited. Consumed by ego, our desires are in fact not simply limited. They are harmful. We're like the child in the following story.

> *A father and his young son were walking down the street. The boy was extremely agitated with his father, shouting, "You're mean, Daddy! Give them to me!" The father held his son's hand tightly and con-*

LIGHT

VS

LIGHT

LIMITED   ENDLESS

tinued walking down the street without response.

Finally, the boy was making such a ruckus, and the father seemed so oblivious to his son, that a passerby felt moved to approach the father and ask him why he treated his son so badly. "Can't you see you're upsetting him?" they complained. "What kind of father denies a son in such distress?"

The father looked patiently at the passerby. "You do not understand," he said. "A few streets back, my son saw some brightly colored pins in a shop window. He wants me to buy them for him so he can play with them. I've told him that the pins are dangerous for a child his age and he risks hurting himself badly."

TRANSFORMING THE DESIRE TO RECEIVE FOR THE SELF ALONE INTO THE DESIRE TO SHARE IS ACTUALLY A SUPREME ACT OF SELF-INTEREST, as long as you spell *Self* with a capital S. This is not the self that is the ego, the self that can only die. I mean the Self that can become one with God, that allows His Light to shine unobstructed forever, because when you are one with God, you *are* like God, with all the rights and privileges of God. The rights of eternal life; the privilege of joy unlimited; the

power to heal, to bless, and to resurrect the dead.

Within the fabric of the universe, there is abundance. In every atom and every cell of life, there is sufficiency. There's nothing wrong, immoral, or ungodly about Self-interest. There's nothing bad about wanting to receive. In fact, the basic attempt to eliminate Self-interest is simply one more trick of the ego. The very reason we pursue transformative sharing is to receive. The word *Kabbalah*, the source of this wisdom, means "to receive." We connect to our godly nature in order to change our vessel into a cup with no bottom so we can receive endlessly.

A sage known as the Master of Kotzk used to tell his students: "You want to know where God's Light is? God's Light is wherever you let Him in." We don't need to pray to God or plead to God for his Light. We just need to remove the walls we've built.

The God Formula is a bulldozer.

WELCOME TO THE STATE OF AMNESIA

You've been wandering in a desert. Years have passed, and your body is caked with hot dry dust. You dream of cool water and fruit, but day after day you survive on nothing but cactus. Cactus in the morning, cactus at night. Then one day a scout arrives with an amazing message: Twenty miles away there's an oasis, with crystal-clear waters, palm trees, and dates.

How do you respond?

There's only one sane response: You drop everything in a nanosecond and race madly in the direction of the oasis. Nothing deters you, nothing distracts you, nothing fills your mind except images of soothing cool water and blissful shade.

With this book, a scout is bringing you news of an oasis. Not only does it offer dates and palms, it holds out eternal joy and fulfillment. What's your response?

Some will say that the scout's mistaken, he's probably seen a mirage. Others will be inspired, head for the oasis, and after a few miles come upon a scrawny palm tree, under which they will proceed to sit for years, insisting that it's the oasis. Others will gather and chat endlessly about the oasis over a nice cup of cactus. Others will claim cacti are the most delicious plants in the world, so who needs an oasis? Most everybody will soon forget that the word *oasis* was ever mentioned.

What on earth is going on?

THE STATE OF EGO IS A STATE OF AMNESIA. WE DON'T REMEMBER WHAT WE CAME HERE TO DO. TO MANIFEST OUR TRUE NATURE AND BECOME LIKE GOD.

So we read something inspirational and are moved by it. Years later, we may stumble upon it by accident and realize we'd totally forgotten about it. We pray or meditate or have life-changing experiences. We feel different. Then we don't. What's up? One moment we have a transformative experience and the next we're cursing the person who bumps into us on the street? Why?

We forget because it's in our nature to forget. Years of living in a consciousness disconnected from God have piled on and covered us like a shell, to the point where our godly nature now is but a pilot light flickering in the vast darkness of egoistic, mechanical behavior.

We need a plan to follow every moment of our lives—right now, this instant, because the next instant we'll forget, and then we'll remember again. The God Formula can't be just another thing we know. It must be remembered constantly with clarity. The assault on ego and the process of transformative sharing must become our operating system: *OS GOD*. **A DROP OF BEING IS WORTH A POUND OF KNOWING.** *Being* is true knowledge, because knowledge without action has limited value. We begin to act; where ego rises up,

VS

we destroy it. When we don't feel like sharing, we share. Each action gets us a little closer to the Light, a little closer to becoming like God, a little further from death.

AND THE MOST IMPORTANT TRUTH OF ALL IS THE FACT THAT BECOMING LIKE GOD *IS* POSSIBLE. We can do it. This is the simplest and most extraordinary truth. **IT IS OBSERVED THAT WE USE ONLY 4 PERCENT OF OUR BRAIN (ON GOOD DAYS). WHO KNOWS HOW MUCH OF OUR HEART AND SOUL WE'RE USING?**

THERE'S AN OASIS NOT FAR AWAY. DON'T FORGET! THIS BOOK IS A STRING TIED AROUND YOUR FINGER; DON'T FORGET! AND EVERY TIME YOU DON'T FORGET, IT GETS A LITTLE EASIER TO REMEMBER.

CHAPTER SIX:

AND DEATH SHALL HAVE NO DOMINION

*There's a story from the Zohar told of the
passing of a sage named Rav Yosi.*

*From the moment of his death, Rav Yosi's
small son was inconsolable, weeping on his
father's bed, pressing his mouth tightly to
his father's mouth, barring anyone from getting near the great sage's body.*

*"Where is the justice?" the boy cried. "I
should have been taken in my father's
place."*

*Refusing consolation, he gripped his father
tightly, as if he believed his small thin arms
were strong enough to resist his father's*

departure to the other world. He implored the heavens to take him instead, and his wails proved so moving that finally a visitor named Rav Elazar began to weep along with the child. He then recited a verse from the Bible. Suddenly a pillar of fire arose and separated the mourners from the dead man, though the child remained attached to the lips of his father.

A voice then spoke to the dead sage: "Blessed are you, Rav Yosi, that the speeches of the young child and his tears rose to the throne of the Holy King. Twenty-two years have been added to your life, so you will have time to teach your son, the perfect and beloved, before the Holy One, blessed be He."

Then the pillar of fire vanished, and Rav Yosi opened his eyes. He saw his son, whose lips remained glued to his, and he heard Rabbi Elazar announce, "Blessed is our lot that we have witnessed the resurrection of the dead."

It is the final taboo. The unthinkable and undeniable. The universal solvent. Death.

KABBALAH COMES TO US FROM A WORLD TO COME, INVITING US TO A NEW COURAGE: NOT

THE COURAGE TO DIE, THE TRADITIONAL MEASURE OF BRAVERY, BUT RATHER, THE COURAGE NOT TO DIE. THE COURAGE TO CONFRONT PHYSICAL IMMORTALITY.

On what basis can we challenge the indisputable truth that we are born to die?

"He will swallow up death forever and God will wipe away the tears of all the faces," says the Bible. It's not possible to read this statement and remain calm. **THE BIBLE PROMISES THE DEATH OF DEATH.**

When Enoch passed on, the Bible says, he did not die. Rather, Enoch was "no longer there because God had taken him," which for Kabbalah means he actually left the earth with his physical body, which did not die.

The Bible also says Elijah did not die but rather was elevated to the upper worlds with his body, rising up to heaven in a chariot of fire.

We challenge the hegemony of death on the basis of such statements in the Bible and truths revealed in the Zohar. The Zohar tells us that **THERE ARE TWO POLES, LIGHT AND DARKNESS. THE LIGHT IS GOD, ETERNAL LIFE, AND TOTAL FULFILLMENT, AND THE DARKNESS IS EGO, OR DESIRE TO RECEIVE FOR THE SELF ALONE, AND IS THE FORCE OF DEATH. WHEN WE CHOOSE TO CONNECT TO DARKNESS, WE**

MOVE CLOSER TOWARD DEATH. WHEN WE CHOOSE TO CONNECT TO THE LIGHT, ON THE OTHER HAND, WE DRAW DOWN MORE AND MORE LIFE FORCE. OUR JOB IS TO TRAVEL TO THE LIGHT. AND WHEN WE REACH IT COMPLETELY, WHEN WE BECOME LIKE GOD, DEATH SHALL HAVE NO DOMINION.

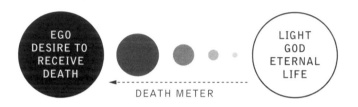

This is the end of death, not on the basis of belief or religious faith or after an apocalypse. We need to make this happen ourselves. The wisdom of the Zohar is here not to strengthen a given belief system but to inspire us to venture beyond belief, to the realm of action, where the deepest human hope travels out of the realm of myth and into the realm of everyday life.

PHYSICAL IMMORTALITY IS POSSIBLE BECAUSE WE HAVE THE POWER TO CREATE IT.

And, knowing that, we have a mandate to make it happen.

It's said in the Zohar that one day Rav Yitzchak approached his friend, Rav Yehuda, with a request: that after he, Rav Yitzchak, goes to his grave, his good friend should pray for him all the seven days of mourning.

Astonished, Rav Yehuda asked why the master supposed he was going to die, whereupon Rav Yitzchak gave two reasons. First, when his soul left him during sleep, it no longer enlightened him with dreams. Second, he no longer saw his shadow. "Once a man's shadow is no longer seen," he reminded his friend, "he passes away from this world."

Rav Yehuda replied, "I shall carry out your requests, but I also ask that you shall reserve a place for me beside you in the other world, just as I was by your side in this world."

Distraught at the prospect of their imminent separation, the two friends finally went to see their master, one of the greatest Kabbalists in history and author of the Zohar, Rav Shimon bar Yochai. Rav Shimon was on such a level in his own journey toward becoming like God that he simply lifted up his eyes and could see the

*angel of death dancing before Rav Yitzchak.
He invited his two students into his home,
but refused entrance to the angel of death.
"Whoever is a usual visitor to my house
shall enter," he said, "and whoever is not
shall be barred." Once inside, Rav Shimon
stood up and said, "Master of the universe,
we have a certain Rav Yitzchak with us.
Behold, I hold him. Give him to me!" A
resounding voice replied, "Behold, Rav
Yitzchak is yours."*

*Rav Yitzchak fell asleep and in his sleep
saw his father, who proclaimed, "Son,
happy is your portion in this world and in
the world to come, for you sit among the
leaves of the tree of life in the Garden of
Eden." A sound went forth in all the worlds:
"Friends who stand here, bedeck yourself for
Rav Shimon who has asked a request of the
Holy One that Rav Yitzchak shall not die,"
and it was granted him.*

*Rav Yitzchak then awoke and laughed. His
face shone.*

If Kabbalist Rav Shimon bar Yochai had the power to
turn back the angel of death with a simple act of will,
why do we invite death into our bedroom so willingly?
Why is the inevitability of death off the table, marked

NOT FOR DISCUSSION? Simply because it has always been that way? Just because we're driving through history with our eyes on the rearview mirror instead of on the road ahead?

Life should come with the same legal disclaimer as financial advertising: PAST PERFORMANCE IS NO GUARANTEE OF FUTURE RESULTS. **TURNING POINTS IN HISTORY ARE NOTHING BUT THE RECORD OF ASSUMPTIONS OVERTHROWN: A DIARY OF IMPOSSIBILITIES AND THOSE WHO ROSE UP TO ACCOMPLISH THEM.** At one time, one-third of humanity died from viruses and bacteria. Today, bubonic plague is just a name for a rock band. At one time, when oil lamps still burned, experts declared that everything that ever would be invented had already been invented. Today, we take and send digital pictures with our cellular telephones.

History is not kind to impossibility. However, impossible physical immortality might seem evolution will sweep that notion aside.

Immortality will not simply happen because we build a time machine, develop stronger antibiotics or download our DNA onto hard drives. Immortality will happen because of our work of becoming like God and because we're already immortal. In our souls, we're already like God, but because we're set apart from God's nature of sharing, we suffer and we die. When we become like God, we erase our own diseases, transform everyday annoyances into opportunities to become free, dismiss the thoughts that cause depression with a wave of our hand, live with a grander purpose than surviving the prison another day, and become the cause of all our experiences. **WE'LL EVEN, LIKE RAV SHIMON BAR YOCHAI, PUT UP A NO TRESPASSING SIGN TO THE ANGEL OF DEATH SO THAT FROM NOW UNTIL ETERNITY, DEATH SHALL HAVE NO DOMINION.**

EGO
DESIRE TO
RECEIVE
DEATH

LIGHT
GOD
ETERNAL
LIFE

DEATH METER

CHAPTER SEVEN

THE OPPONENT: THE STUFF THAT DEATH IS MADE OF

IT'S NOT US. IT'S HIM.

He's a deadly parasite, a prison guard who prevails, not by putting us in a cell, but by putting himself inside us. He's a dark force moving inside our bodies, thinking inside our brains, and commanding our actions endlessly, all with the aim of our total and absolute annihilation.

WE DON'T LIVE. HE LIVES US.

Ancient Kabbalists called the Opponent the *evil inclination*. Evil, because of the ruthless campaign of confusion, forgetfulness, doubt, and despair with which he carpet bombs our souls. Evil, because he hotwires us to the Desire to Receive for the Self Alone. Evil, because he's a force pervading the universe, at work 24/7 to block our true nature and imprison us in pain, suffering, and death.

WE DON'T LIVE. HE LIVES US.

THE OPPONENT HAS US CONVINCED THAT WE'RE FREE INDIVIDUALS, WHEREAS 99% OF OUR THOUGHTS ARE HIS. HE HAS CONVINCED US THAT THE EGO SELF IS OUR GREATEST FRIEND WHEN, IN FACT, IT'S OUR FIERCEST ENEMY. He's the reason we live in what is external to our God nature—ego—rather than in our essence, which is the Desire to Share.

So, one day, we're inspired by a piece of wisdom. It resonates deep within us like an ancient memory. We're intrigued, inquisitive. Then suddenly we remember a parking ticket we forgot to pay. Then we realize we're a little hungry and wonder if we should have a snack. In minutes, we've forgotten the wisdom. This is no accident. **IT'S NOT US. IT'S HIM.** Then we remember. *I could actually be free of suffering and death*, we think to ourselves. Then a voice inside says, "Don't be naïve." **IT'S NOT US. IT'S HIM.** "No one escapes," the conversation in our minds continues. "Don't delude yourself. Life is suffering and then you die. Anyone who says differently is in it for the profit. You're depressed, but at least you're not a sucker." **IT'S NOT US. IT'S HIM.**

IT'S NOT US. IT'S HIM.

This is a snapshot of prison life. This is the Opponent hard at work, manning the gates.

He lives in our bodies, and we aren't even angry about it. Instead, we focus on looking good, not understanding that this desire makes us slaves to everyone who sees us. **IT'S NOT US. IT'S HIM.** We curse the driver who cuts us off at the intersection, not understanding that we're sacrificing our health, our sense of well-being on this morning of our lives to someone we've never met. **IT'S NOT US** who wants to yell from the car window. **IT'S HIM.**

It gets worse. Desire to Receive for the Self Alone means permanent war with the physical world. The Opponent convinces us that we're entitled to comfort, and then tells us we should be irritated when everything doesn't go our way. Again, **IT'S NOT US. IT'S THE OPPONENT.**

We believe we're the active principle in our lives, but we're reacting constantly. We don't control. We are controlled.

IT'S NOT US. IT'S HIM.

And now we never need to be fooled again by anger or depression or fear. Because every time we're about to act, or react, we'll ask, **"IS IT ME OR IS IT HIM?"** and we'll know it's us if it's moving us closer to becoming like God.

WHY DO YOU ASK MY NAME?

In the book of Genesis, Jacob wrestles with an angel who is the sum of all the negative energy in the universe. Jacob eventually defeats him, and as the angel begs for release, Jacob issues him a challenge: "I'll let you go if you tell me your name."

The angel replies: "Why do you ask my name?"

It seems an innocent question. But within this question Kabbalists see a secret to unraveling the power of the dark force.

A person's name is his or her essence. When Jacob demands the angel's name, he's demanding to know his essence. What is the wellspring of the Opponent's power? How is he so able to dominate people? If Jacob can understand his essence, he can defeat him. "Why do you ask my name?" the angel replies, and in that question, Kabbalists believe Jacob got his answer.

His name is *Why do you ask my name?* That's his name.
THAT'S HIS ESSENCE. THE POWER OF CONFUSION. THE POWER TO MAKE PEOPLE DOUBT, TO QUESTION WHY THEY EVEN BOTHER TO FIGURE THINGS OUT.

FOCUS AND CLARITY ARE THE OPPONENT'S MORTAL ENEMIES. WE MUST FIGHT FOR CLARITY EVERY MOMENT: CLARITY ABOUT

YOU
(YOU - EGO + SHARING = GOD)

SHARING
YOU
DOING

WALL (OPPONENT)

THE IMPORTANCE OF CLARITY, CLARITY THAT WE'RE IN A PRISON, CLARITY THAT THERE'S A GOD FORMULA TO BE APPLIED, CLARITY THAT WE'RE DESTINED TO BE LIKE GOD.

If life is asleep in us, courtesy of the sedative called Desire to Receive for the Self Alone, Jacob's tussle with the angel represents our struggle to wake up. Most of the time, whenever people have attempted to think clearly throughout history, the angel has wrestled them into submission.

We live in the Reign of Confusion, presided over by the angel *Why do you ask my name?*

WALL (OPPONENT)

One of his greatest allies is a principle of physical existence called the gap between cause and effect. There's no effect without a cause, and no cause without effect. And were there no gap between cause and effect, were we instantly to see the results of our actions, we'd see clearly what needed to be done. But the gap between cause and effect erects a wall of blindness between our selfish actions and the Darkness that ensues. So, one morning we might be impatient with someone at work. No big deal. Two weeks later we wake up in a bad mood and wonder why. "It's just my nature," we may say. "I'm just an unhappy person. I need a double espresso." What we don't see is the correlation between an act of selfishness two weeks ago and a negative result this morning.

Time doesn't heal all wounds, it just obscures their cause. **IF WE COULD SEE THAT EVERY ACTION ARISING FROM THE DESIRE TO RECEIVE FOR THE SELF ALONE HAS A NEGATIVE CONSEQUENCE, WE'D ARISE FROM OUR SLUMBER. WE'D REALIZE THAT OUR ACTIONS HAVE CONSEQUENCES, AS SURE AS THE SUN RISES, AND THAT WE HAVE THE POWER TO CHANGE THOSE CONSEQUENCES.**

CAUSE
ACTION

EFFECT
CONSEQUENCE

TIME

We have the power to be proactive, not reactive. Once we see the connection between actions and results, it becomes easier to change. With correlation comes correction. And with correction comes power. The Opponent fears our power most of all, so he convinces us that we're insignificant.

CAUSE
ACTION

EFFECT
CONSEQUENCE

TIME

In the Reign of Confusion, with the angel *Why do you ask my name?* presiding on every corner, we must be steadfast in our desire for clarity and focus. Clarity and focus transform our actions. **WHEN WE GIVE CHARITY FOR THE PURPOSE OF BEING A GOOD PERSON, WE FEEL GOOD. WHEN WE GIVE CHARITY FOR THE PURPOSE OF BECOMING LIKE GOD, WE BECOME IMMORTAL.**

Such are the stakes of the battle. **THE OPPONENT DOES NOT REST. HE HAS NO PAID HOLIDAYS. HE NEVER RUNS HOME TO CATCH MUST-SEE TV. LOOK UP, AND HE'LL BE THERE.** So, whatever victories we win, they're not opportunities to take a rest but platforms from which to battle further.

THE NAME OF DEATH

EGO IS THE STUFF OF WHICH DEATH IS MADE.

Ego is the Desire to Receive for the Self Alone, a serpent bite that poured venom into Adam and Eve in the Garden of Eden and has flowed through human veins ever since. That is our foundation story, the angel of death convincing Adam and Eve to eat of the tree of knowledge. We carry the venom of the serpent, or ego, with us now. We are led along a path of more and more selfishness until things reach a critical mass and an angel bearing a new name shows up: the angel of death. "You have completed your journey to me," he says. "Now you are mine."

EGO IS THE ENERGY OF DEATH. When we connect to the Creator, we remove death from our lives. It begins by realizing, by making real inside our beings, that **EVERY TIME WE GO AFTER THE DESIRE TO RECEIVE FOR THE SELF ALONE, WE'RE ACTUALLY ATTRACTING DEATH.** When we see this as an absolute fact, we'll get closer to becoming like God.

The Opponent has prevented us from putting cause and effect together, the true correlation between what we do and what we experience. We don't see that the Desire to Receive for the Self Alone leads to pain, suffering, and ultimately, death. This allows us to pretend that a selfish action has no consequence. The venom flows. We can choose the self alone every minute of every day for 80 years, millions of tiny decisions over a lifetime, and when our negativity has accumulated to a critical point, we die.

Or we can start removing the venom.

Drop by drop.

CHAPTER EIGHT

COMFORT KILLS

It's the potion that lets us drift thoughtlessly and robotically toward death.

It's a deadly drug, sold throughout the prison, flowing through the veins of its prisoners.

The drug is comfort.

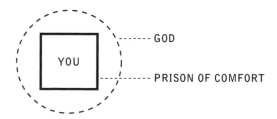

Comfort is the illusion that we're getting somewhere while the treadmill turns and the clock ticks. **COMFORT IS A WARM BLANKET THAT KEEPS US WRAPPED IN THE DESIRE TO RECEIVE FOR THE SELF ALONE, OBLIVIOUS TO THE URGENT NEED TO CHANGE.**

"I'm comfortable. This prison really isn't all that bad. Perhaps the goal of life is for us all to have a productive stay in prison. One day I may even grow up to be president of the cell block. It could happen. It's a free prison."

Or,

"I'm comfortable. You know, maybe I'm not even in prison. Maybe I've been hallucinating all this time. Maybe I'm in the South Seas and these concrete walls are really sand and the bare light bulb is a warm, glowing sun."

Comfort kills, even though seeking it is a biologically determined survival strategy. Organisms instinctively flee discomfort; that's why they survive. **BUT WHAT'S COMFORTABLE FOR THE BODY IS MISERY FOR THE SOUL. AS SOULS, WE'RE TRAPPED IN THE 24-HOUR SURVIVAL DRAMA OF THE BODIES WE INHABIT.** The comfort we truly long for, the ultimate and only comfort, is union with the Creator.

On the one hand we have the illusory comfort of the body, then, and on the other, the true comfort of the

soul. We cannot be comfortable in both universes at the same time, any more than we can go east while we're going west. We're either moving toward God or we're moving toward ego, death, and suffering. And the road to real comfort—which is God—passes through a great deal of discomfort.

It passes through discomfort because it mandates destruction of the need to feel special, the hunger for approval, the longing to belong, the addiction to the fluff of flattery—all the mental junk food, empty of real nutrition, that we stuff into our brains to feed the illusion of an ego self.

THE JOURNEY TO GOD IS AN EJECTION SEAT FROM THE COMFORT ZONE. If the signpost reads DISCOMFORT, we know we're on the right road. When we go against our human nature, we're on the right road. When someone bruises our ego and instead of walking out indignantly as is customary, we stay and study the pain, we welcome the bruising, and we feel gratitude to the insulters, to those who've given us this opportunity to bring more Light and less comfort into our lives, then we're on the right road.

We define comfort as the absence of pain. But **TRUE COMFORT IS THE CROSSING OF AN ABYSS. ON ONE SIDE IS US. ON THE OTHER IS FULFILLMENT. WE'VE BEEN TRYING TO DRAG HAPPINESS OVER TO OUR SIDE OF THE ABYSS, WHEN WHAT WE REALLY NEED TO DO**

IS JUMP TO THE OTHER SIDE. LEAPING THE ABYSS IS TOTAL TRANSFORMATION OF OUR NATURE: BECOMING LIKE THE CREATOR RATHER THAN HOPING THE CREATOR WILL BECOME LIKE US.

A famous Kabbalist described it this way: We're trying to transform God's desires to ours, so He'll give us what we want. But God's desires are what we actually need, so we should make our desires conform to His. When one student complained that he had prayed over and over but God had not answered his prayers, the Kabbalist replied, "God has answered your prayers. The answer was no."

When we're uncomfortable, the prison bars weaken. When we share when it's uncomfortable to share, we're pounding a battering ram against the walls. When we welcome humiliation, the prison door strains at its hinges.

SO IF WE WOULD SEEK TO BECOME LIKE GOD, WE MUST SEEK THE UNCOMFORTABLE

—with a myriad of small steps each leading in the same direction: out of the comfort zone.

THE LESSON OF THE CLOWN SUIT

A famous Kabbalist was out walking one day when he turned to his companion and said, "The wonderful smell of the Garden of Eden is coming from this house. Let's investigate."

They went inside the house. The Kabbalist explained to the owner why they had stopped and asked if they could look around to discover what was producing such an intoxicating smell. The man agreed, delighted to receive two such renowned sages.

The Kabbalist and the others walked from room to room, eventually reaching the man's bedroom. The Kabbalist went to the closet and, asking to look inside, found, hidden way in back behind shoes and boxes, a clown suit. The Kabbalist picked up the suit and announced, "This is the source of the fragrance of the Garden of Eden that fills this house and even the street outside. Sir, would you be so kind as to tell us the story of this costume?"

The man went red in the face. "I really wish you hadn't brought this up," he said. "I've been trying to forget about it for a long time! But I'll tell you the story.

"A few years ago, one of the townspeople came to me desperate for some money to help him breathe a little while he paid off some debts. I told him I'd do everything I could.

"Since I had little money of my own at the time, I knocked on all the doors in my neighborhood, asking for money to help a man in such a wretched situation. Very few of my neighbors contributed anything, and at the end of six or seven hours of traveling from house to house, I had barely scraped any money together at all.

"It was now late in the evening and, quite weary, I walked to the local tavern for some refreshment, wondering what more I could do to help the poor man. Despondent, I looked in my purse, but there wasn't enough to make even a dent in his debts.

"At the next table, a group of wealthy men were laughing and slapping one another on the back rowdily, evidently quite drunk. One of them leaned over to me, a strong smell of beer on his breath, and asked, 'Why are you looking so glum?' I told him the whole story and he said, 'I have an idea. I'll give you

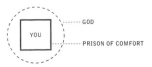

the money, but you have to do something for me. I have this clown suit and I want you to put it on and walk with me through the town. What a hoot that will be!'

"I looked at him aghast. 'But it's after midnight,' I stammered. 'We'll wake everyone up.'

"The man roared with laughter. 'That's the whole point,' he said.

"Well, the streets of our town are more alleyways than streets, and the townsfolk all like to keep their bedroom windows open at night. It was clear that we were about to start a riot. I thought that if I was able to rush through the town quickly enough to avoid being lynched, perhaps it wouldn't be such a big price to pay to get the money I needed. I finally looked up at the man and said, 'Okay. I'll do it.'

"What I had not bargained for was that the man was going to bring all his drinking companions to join the fun. So there we were, parading through the town, 30 drunks singing and screaming, and me out in front in the clown suit, hoping the earth would open and swallow me up.

"Lights went on everywhere. Irate men and women in their nightclothes looked out their windows and shouted obscenities at us. More than a few emptied their chamber pots. This went on for over an hour, by which time there wasn't a man, woman, or child in the town who hadn't witnessed my utter disgrace.

"Finally, the drunks had had enough. The man paid me my money and I rushed home, my face burning with shame. I threw the clown suit into the back of my closet and did everything I could to forget that night—the worst I'd ever had."

When the man had finished his story, the Kabbalist looked at him with bright eyes. "That explains why this extraordinary fragrance was coming from your closet," he said. "Your sharing action shattered your ego so completely that a tremendous amount of Light was revealed. Indeed, so powerful is the protection that even after your death it will continue. Tell your family to bury you in the suit when you die, for it will give you immediate admission into the Garden of Eden."

The story of the clown suit is a PhD-level seminar in ego destruction. The suit offered discomfort powerful

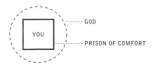

enough to grant its wearer instant admission to the Garden of Eden.

But for most of us, becoming like God will probably not be the result of one grand gesture. It will come in countless small victories, taking us step by step out of the prison cell of comfort. By actively seeking the uncomfortable, we awaken our divine nature. **UNDER EVERY ROCK OF DISCOMFORT IS CONCEALED AN OPPORTUNITY TO BECOME LIKE GOD.**

THE QUESTION IS NOT, AM I TAKING SPIRITUAL ACTION? THE QUESTION IS, AM I TAKING UNCOMFORTABLE ACTION?

We challenge the Opponent in his personal fiefdom, the comfort zone, aware of his big lie. Contrary to what he promises, when we seek comfort before transformation, we'll never be truly at ease. On the other hand, when becoming like God is our sole objective, we'll find ultimate peace.

This book must make you uncomfortable, or it has failed in its mission. It's a personal invitation to the ultimate comfort that awaits on the other side of discomfort.

It is the fight of your life.

It is the fight *for* your life.

CHAPTER NINE:

"THE HEART OF MISGUIDED PEOPLE IS ALMOST"

When we're in a maximum-security prison, an escape plan is not escapist reading. It is not just something to while away the time lying on our bunks. If it's a true escape plan, it will enflame our dreams of freedom and dominate our every waking moment. This is where a physical prison differs from the prison we call life. Because in the prison of life, chained to ego, a human being may well stumble upon an escape plan—perhaps in the gray dungeon light, read of a path to eternal light. What will be his response? Most likely he'll pursue the escape plan for years, each day venturing out from his cell to gather more information, then returning each night to regale fellow prisoners with what he learned. He'll never actually leave the prison, but he'll comfort himself for years with the notion that he's truly on the road of escape.

What chains human beings to the mediocrity of *almost*? Lack of clarity of our purpose in this world, and lack of clarity about the true scope and power of the God Formula keep us enslaved. Once becoming like God is clearly seen as the only goal, we cannot possibly be satisfied with simply sharing, meditating, praying, or doing good. **OUR GOAL IS NOT TO BE GOOD. IT'S TO BECOME LIKE GOD.** Rather than a hobby, the journey to becoming like God is nothing less than a wholehearted struggle conducted every second that we breathe.

OUR TRANSFORMATION TO GOD IS THE ONLY WORTHWHILE GOAL IN LIFE. NOTHING LESS THAN COMPLETION OF THE JOURNEY WILL DO. But we inhabit a mentality where completeness doesn't exist, where C is passing, where 51% is a majority, where comfort is the goal.

THE ILLUSION OF THE MIDDLE

Understanding the God Formula shatters what I call the illusion of the middle. This illusion tells us that somewhere between an all-out assault on the Desire to Receive for the Self Alone and a life of utter Darkness, there's a pleasant garden of mediocrity. A peaceful place for us to watch TV, give to charity, think about spirituality, and build our 401(k) retirement funds.

Shattering the illusion leads to the realization that

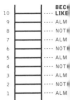

there is no middle. **WE'RE EITHER ON THE ROAD TO LIGHT OR WE'RE ON THE ROAD TO DARKNESS. WE'RE EITHER BECOMING LIKE GOD OR WE'RE COMMITTING SUICIDE. THERE IS NO OTHER POSITION.** We may reject this as melodrama, and the Opponent hopes that we do. But when we continue living in ego nature, obsessed with our self, when we purr at compliments and bristle when not paid the proper respect, when we fulfill selfish desires without regard to the pain of others, we're slowly committing suicide. We're opting for the Desire to Receive for the Self Alone. At a crossroads, we're choosing the sign marked PAIN, SUFFERING, AND DEATH.

On the other hand, **WHEN WE CRUSH THE FORCE OF EGO, WHEN WE EXPERIENCE HUMILIATION AND THANK THE HUMILIATOR FOR THE OPPORTUNITY, WHEN WE SHARE SO THAT IT HURTS, ESPECIALLY IF THAT SHARING IS THE LAST THING WE WANT TO DO, WE'RE STEPPING INTO IMMORTALITY. WE'RE BECOMING LIKE GOD.**

And we either complete that journey, or we're nowhere.

> *There once was a master whose time had come to leave this world. He summoned his many students to his deathbed. One by one, they bent over his frail body and listened*

intently as he told them what their special tasks would be when he was gone. Finally, it was the turn of one of the master's closest students, whom the master had known and loved for many years.

"Your job," the wise man whispered to him, "is to travel all over the world and tell stories about my life that will inspire people to seek the truth."

The student was disappointed. In those days it was a hardship to travel great distances, and besides, he would miss his friends and family during his long absences. However, he understood that the highest good for everyone, himself included, would come from fulfilling his divine purpose in life, so he was determined to obey the instruction. He kissed his master's hand and asked, "Will this be my duty forever or only for a certain time?"

"You will know when you've completed your job," the master replied.

For many years, the student traveled from city to city and from country to country, telling stories about his master's life. Being a gifted raconteur, he invariably lifted up the hearts of his audience and left them

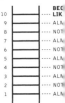

resolved to grow spiritually. Though he experienced the deep satisfaction that comes from fulfilling his purpose, he longed to receive a sign that would announce the completion of his mission.

One day, he heard of a very wealthy man, living in a faraway town, who was reputed to pay handsomely anyone who could tell him authentic stories about the master. The student decided to embark on the long journey in the hope of improving his finances, which were in a sorry state. He arrived in the town a few days later and went straight to the wealthy man's house.

"I was at the master's side continuously for many years," he told the man, "and I know thousands of stories."

That evening, the household gathered around the dining room table and all eyes were upon the student.

"Speak to us," the wealthy man said. "I believe you may know a story that I have waited a long time to hear."

The student opened his mouth to speak, but he could think of nothing to say. His mind had gone completely blank. Over the years,

*he'd told countless stories, yet now he could
not remember even one of them.*

*The wealthy man tried to hide his disap-
pointment and told the student not to worry.
"Perhaps you need sleep," he suggested.
"We'll talk again in the morning." However,
the next day the same thing happened. The
student's mind went totally blank. He
flushed and stammered out an apology, sure
that the family must suspect him of tricking
them in order to enjoy their hospitality.
Then he quickly rode away, vowing never to
revisit the town that had been the setting for
such an ordeal. After traveling for four or
five hours, however, something made him
stop in his tracks: He suddenly remembered
a story. He wrestled with himself for a few
moments.*

*"Should I go back?" he wondered. "It's not
much of a story. By the time I return it will
be late and I'll be tired. Besides, the man
will have me arrested if I start banging on
his door in the middle of the night claiming
I remember a story."*

*The student then recalled the man's excite-
ment when he thought the student could tell
him stories, and the bitter disappointment
on his face when he realized their time*

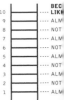

118

together would be fruitless; and the student remembered his master's sacred instruction to bring inspiration to people around the world. At length, he turned his reluctant horse around and started the journey back to the wealthy man's town. He arrived at the man's house after midnight and knocked at the door, which was instantly opened. The man stood in the doorway and the student noticed that the man's eyes were red, as though he'd been crying for a long time.

"I remember a story!" the student exclaimed. "But it's one of the poorest stories in my repertoire. It's based on my own experience and I don't even know how it turns out. I can only recount a fragment."

"Never mind," the man said, ushering the traveler into the living room and beckoning him to sit down. A servant brought tea, and the wealthy man could barely contain himself while the student refreshed himself with a few sips of the drink. Finally, the student began his story.

"Once there was a town ruled by a cruel governor. My master heard that this man had planned a massacre for the next day, and so my master set off across the forest with his entourage in order to visit the governor and see if he could stop it. When we reached the town, my master summoned me and told me to go talk to the governor and arrange a meeting with him. I looked at my master aghast.

"'He'll kill me,' I stammered.

"'Just go and do as I say,' my master replied serenely.

"I requested an audience with the governor and explained to him that my master wished to see him at the inn where my master had taken a room. The governor sat in an immense leather chair, almost like a throne, and pondered for a moment. There were a dozen guards protecting him, all armed with gleaming scimitars. It appeared certain that he would nod to them and I would be instantly hacked to pieces. But to my surprise, the governor glanced up at me and informed me that he would visit my master at once.

"The governor and my master met for several hours, but I never learned what they discussed. All I know is that, as a result of the meeting, the governor called off the impending massacre. Soon afterward, he left the town and was never heard from again.

That's all I can tell you."

The wealthy man rose and embraced the student, all the while crying like a baby.

"That was me," the man said. "I was the governor. I had lived a terrible life and killed many innocent people. I thought there was no hope for me, until I met your master. Somehow, he was able to reach my soul. He told me many things that stirred me deeply, and I resolved immediately to change my ways. I asked him if there was any hope for me, and he told me that there was. The master then gave me exact instructions for cleansing myself of my evil deeds. Then I asked him, 'How will I know when I have completed my correction?'

"He replied, 'If ever a man comes to you and tells you your story, then you'll know that you are absolved.'"

The wealthy man hugged the student again and said, "That's why for all these years I've been paying a fortune to hear stories about the master, in the hope of hearing my own. After you left last night, I understood what was happening: You were the bearer of the master's story and I had been offered a chance to finish my correction, but I had missed it. I began praying, crying, and begging for help in cleansing myself of any last residue of my past. My prayers must have been answered, for you remembered the story and you came back."

This story is about a moment in time when two men choose to go the extra mile and, in doing so, achieve their ultimate purpose. The wealthy man could have accepted his disappointment and gone to bed. The student could have kept on his way. He was exhausted, he was ashamed, and it was getting late. It would have been easy to push on to the night's lodging. Most people would have.

The secret of completion is to eradicate *almost*. To get rid of *good enough and close enough*. To Rav Ashlag, the greatest pain was seeing people who had begun their journey but failed to complete it. The rest of the world didn't bother him, all those millions who never embarked on the journey to God, who never even bothered to glance from the windows of the prison. But he suffered deeply when someone struggled on the journey and fell short.

Rav Ashlag spoke often about persistence. He would say, **"THERE'S A TREASURE IN YOUR ATTIC, AND A LADDER WITH TEN RUNGS LEADING UP TO IT. YOU STOP AT THE NINTH RUNG. YOU MAY THINK YOU WENT FAR. THE**

WORLD MAY THINK YOU WENT FAR. BUT
YOU'RE ONLY ON THE NINTH RUNG. YOU'VE
GAINED NOTHING."

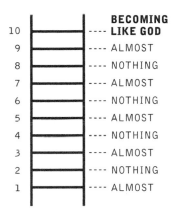

TO ALL OF HUMANITY WHO'VE STOPPED ON
THE NINTH RUNG, THE MESSAGE IS SIMPLE:
YOU ASKED THE WRONG QUESTION. YOU
ASKED, HOW SPIRITUAL AM I? WHEN THE
REAL QUESTION IS, AM I LIKE GOD YET?

Becoming like God does not fit into our schedules. It's
very inconvenient, in fact. It forces us to subordinate all
other agendas. It has no days off. But we come to realize that, with our souls hanging in the balance, the dis-
tractions of life are nothing less than insanity. Pursuing
them is like watching TV while the house burns down.

**UNWAVERING EFFORT IS THE REQUIREMENT
OF TRANSFORMATION.** We can try tapping gently

on a board for a hundred years and not break it. But if we focus all of our force in a single, wholehearted blow, the board will shatter. Praying, meditating, volunteering for charity, and pursuing excellence are fine pursuits. But if they don't result in actual transformation, in becoming like God, they're almost pointless.

A story is told in the Bible about Rebecca. During her pregnancy, she noticed something quite strange: Whenever she passed by certain parts of town—a place of study or prayer—she felt her child wanting to go there. At the same time, whenever she passed by other parts of town—a house of idol worshippers or a den of thieves—she felt her child wanting to go there also. The phenomenon worried her, because she thought her child might be hesitating over whether to follow the path of evil or the path of righteousness.

She decided to go to a wise man for advice, and he told her, "You are carrying two children. One twin is going to be a spiritual giant, and the other is going to be drawn to darkness." He was referring to her two sons, Jacob and Esau.

Upon hearing this news, Rebecca had an astonishing reaction: She was not in

the least bit dismayed. She was delighted.

THE EXTRAORDINARY LESSON OF THIS STORY IS THAT FOR MOST OF US, BEING GOOD IS A BARRIER TO BECOMING LIKE GOD.

Average will never rise above average, but extreme darkness carries within it the potential to see its darkness and change. Thus Rebecca was delighted that neither of her children were destined for mediocrity, doomed never to become like God. One child was perfect, one totally negative. In their extremes, both escaped the dangers of mediocrity. Both had strong potential to become like God.

These are the truths that can set us free. The problem with these truths, as with all truths, is that it's not enough simply to read them. It's not enough simply to understand them. We need to own them. **WHAT WE NEED TO DO IS MAKE THE GOD FORMULA A PART OF OUR CELLS, TO LET IT ENTER OUR DNA AND CHANGE OUR BASIC CODING.**

AS KING SOLOMON SAID, "THE HEART OF MISGUIDED PEOPLE IS 'ALMOST.'" The road may seem impossible, yet it's our destiny to transform our nature. Ultimately, we'll all achieve it. The only question is, How long will we postpone this, the journey back to God, who is closer than the air we breathe, present constantly until the journey is completed.

CHAPTER TEN:
WEAPONS OF WAR

We're proposing escape from the greatest maximum security prison ever built. So it is not simply a matter of sneaking out when the guard is sleeping. In this prison, the guard never sleeps.

Escape from the prison of life is more akin to armed combat. The Zohar calls our life a war zone, a ceaseless battle against a negative force that operates inside our skin, inside our brain, inside our cells, consigns us to robotic existence, and then kills us as a reward. It is mortal combat in the cause of immortal life.

We inhabit a war zone, we who would walk through the door that has opened at this moment in human consciousness. **WE ARE EITHER REACTIVE, MECHANICAL, PUPPETS OF THE OPPONENT,**

OR WE ARE PRO-ACTIVE AGENTS OF OUR OWN GODLY NATURE. We are either one or the other. Each moment of existence, we have a choice of operating system, and every moment is an opportunity to upgrade. There is joy with each revealment of Light, but the reality of war continues nevertheless, **THE UNDERLYING BATTLE NEVER ENDS UNTIL WE BECOME LIKE GOD.**

So this book can be looked at in another way: it is an arsenal of weapons. lying ready in the battle for our soul, on a battleground called our life.

RECOGNITION is the first weapon. We must recognize it is a prison we inhabit and not a luxury hotel, because recognition breeds urgency and only in urgency can the fervor for escape begin.

REFUSAL is the second weapon. Only in refusing to accept death and suffering as final realities can the power to act begin.

THE GOD FORMULA is the third weapon. Only with absolute clarity and focus on the ultimate goal and the means of getting there can we break through the walls and become like God.

UNMASKING THE OPPONENT is the fourth weapon, because he will trick, confuse and deceive at every turn.

CERTAINTY is the fifth weapon. Only with certainty of the extraordinary potential of every human being to become like God can our goal be achieved.

VIGILANCE AGAINST COMFORT is the sixth weapon, because only by turning away from the death-trap of comfort and plunging gladly into the realm of discomfort can we begin the destruction of the ego and transformative sharing.

COMPLETION is the seventh weapon, because only with ceaseless focus and remembrance of the ultimate goal, and refusal to settle for anything less than total transformation, will we become like God.

HATING EGO

Rav Ashlag once shocked his students.

"None of you truly believe what I have taught you about the ego," he told them. "If you had believed me, you would have changed by now."

You would have changed by now.

Even after years of work with a great Kabbalist, the indefatigable ego resists conquest.

Why haven't we changed by now? What's the secret to the durability of the Desire to Receive for the Self

Alone? Why is our devotion to ego so unswerving? The simple answer is, We don't hate it enough. We don't find the evils unleashed by ego sufficiently repugnant to do what's necessary to transform. The Opponent has hypnotized us to believe the care and feeding of ego is in our best interests—even as it ends our lives. **IN THIS BATTLE, OUR ADVANTAGE LIES IN THE NATURE OF OUR ESSENCE TO AUTOMATICALLY REJECT ANYTHING IT PERCEIVES AS NEGATIVE. SO, IT'S VITALLY IMPORTANT TO RECOGNIZE NEGATIVITY. OUR WORK IS NOT SO MUCH GETTING RID OF THE NEGATIVITY, AS IT IS MERELY SEEING IT. THE PROCESS OF SEEING IT IS SYNONYMOUS WITH DISPELLING IT.**

IF PEOPLE REALLY KNEW THAT EVERY TIME THEY GOT ANGRY THEY WERE COMMITTING SUICIDE, THEY'D NEVER GET ANGRY AGAIN. This makes the journey to becoming like God more about seeing and less about doing. And being continually shocked at each new piece of ego we see, even as the whole world praises us for our humility.

How much should we abhor ego?

Someone once approached a great Kabbalist. "I have to tell you that, a few months ago, one of your students acted in the most disgusting way," he said.

Hearing the student's name, the Kabbalist replied, "Zushya is one of the most spiritual people you could ever meet. I cannot believe he acted badly. Tell me the story."

"Well, there was to be a wedding in our town," the man related, "and on the day of the ceremony, the mother of the bride lost the dowry. The whole town had been excited about the wedding, but now that it had to be canceled, everyone was sad and some people were arguing and fighting—it was awful. Suddenly, this man entered the wedding hall, introduced himself as Zushya, and announced that he had found the dowry. You can imagine how relieved everybody was, especially the bride and her family. We were all delighted, but soon our delight turned to outrage. Zushya went on to say, 'If you want the dowry back, you must pay me a 20 percent finder's fee.'

"We stared at him in astonishment. 'Are you insane?' I said. 'What kind of man would ask for a finder's fee in these circumstances? Just give the money back to her.' But he insisted that he would not return the money without first taking his 20 percent finder's fee.

"Things went from bad to worse. A brawl

started. The bride's family beat Zushya and grabbed the money from his pockets. Then the rest of us got hold of him and ran him out of town. And, frankly, I can't really say that what we did was wrong, because what type of rogue would act in that way?"

The Kabbalist said, "There must be some explanation for this. Let me talk to Zushya and find out what happened."

"It was like this," Zushya explained. "My daughter was supposed to get married and, being a poor man, I didn't have funds for her dowry, so I traveled from town to town to make some money. After two months of hard work, I had finally collected the sum I needed and was on my way home when I came through this town in which everyone was so sad and forlorn. I asked what had happened and they told me the story of the lost dowry. I decided to do a great act of sharing and give the bride's family the money I'd collected for my daughter. I found out exactly how much money was lost, and in what denominations, and I planned to hand it over to the family and pretend I had found it. However, as I was walking toward the wedding hall, the Opponent suddenly started talking to me. 'Zushya,' he said, ' you are such a good

HATE EGO, SHARE RIDICULOUSLY NOW. AND NOW. AND NOW.

guy. Who else in the world would do what you're doing? You don't have any money, you've worked hard for months to collect money for your daughter's wedding, and here you are giving it to the family of someone else's daughter whom you don't even know. You must be the most sharing person in the world.'

"The Opponent went on and on like this, and I could feel my ego growing and growing, so I said to myself, 'I want to do this act of sharing with this family, but I cannot possibly let my ego take all the credit in this way.' So, I looked for a means of giving the money to the bride's family while at the same time giving my ego a good bashing. That's how I came up with the idea of demanding a 20 percent finder's fee. I knew they would never give it to me and that I would be run out of town in disgrace."

The ego dictates. It told the man in the story not to give his money away. Then it told him to take credit for his generosity. But Zushya was at war, and hatred of ego was a weapon that didn't falter.

RIDICULOUS SHARING

When we live in ego nature, sharing is an unnatural act. Sharing violates the ego's fundamental survival need: I want it for myself. This is a deep, dark pit, an unscratchable itch, a bottomless longing destined never to be filled.

Becoming like God begins with behaving *like* God, and that means transforming into a being of sharing. It's logical, then, that if sharing is the route to transformation and transformation is the escape route from death and suffering, we'd rush to share with the ardor of a convict making a prison break. We'd see a person in need of help much as an inmate sees a metal file. **THE MORE WE SHARE, THE CLOSER WE GET TO THE SUNSHINE BEYOND THE PRISON WALLS. THE MORE UNCOMFORTABLE THE SHARING, THE FASTER WE GET THERE.** It's the principle of growth. The barbell we lift easily doesn't build strength as quickly as the barbell lifted with struggle. Being kind, giving to charity, and handing out money to beggars are all acts of sharing embedded safely in our comfort zone, so the biceps of our godly nature grow only a little. **SHARING UNREASONABLY, UNEXPECTEDLY, WHEN IT'S A SACRIFICE TO DO SO, WHEN IT GOES AGAINST OUR NATURE TO DO SO, WHEN SOMEONE COMPLIMENTS US ON OUR FAVORITE PEN AND WE SAY, "TAKE IT" —** *THAT'S* **WHEN WE START TO BECOME LIKE GOD.**

HATE EGO, SHARE RIDICULOUSLY
NOW. AND NOW. AND NOW.

In the Bible, Abraham wanted to find a wife for his son, Isaac, so he sent his servant, Elazar, to a certain town to look for the right woman. The servant took ten camels with him and, when he arrived at the town, he made them kneel down at a well at early evening, the time when women came out to draw water. He prayed to God, "May you so arrange it that the maiden to whom I shall say, 'Please tip over your jug so that I may drink,' and who replies, 'Drink and I will even water your camels,' shall be the appointed daughter-in-law for my master.

No sooner had he finished praying than a beautiful maiden, Rebecca, appeared with a jug upon her shoulder. She descended to the spring, and Elazar ran to her and said, "Let me please sip a little water from your jug."

She replied, "Please drink your fill," and when she had finished giving him to drink, she said, "I will draw water even for your camels until they have finished drinking."

Immediately, Elazar understood that his prayer had been answered and that he had found Isaac's soul mate.

The story of Rebecca is a representation of transformative sharing. It's easy to offer water to a stranger; it's absurd to offer water for his entire camel herd. Unless the action has conscious intent behind it, the intent is to awaken the divinity within oneself. Then, the sharing is done for oneself and not for the receiver. Rebecca was operating on the level of conscious intent to become like God and was thus found to be a worthy partner for Isaac.

What distinguishes ordinary sharing from transformative sharing has nothing to do with what's being shared. The consciousness and the difficulty behind the act determine its payload of Light. A dollar given with the conscious desire to grow, to become like God, is an act of transformative sharing. A bequest of ten million dollars, given for self-glorification, fame, and additional power, is not. **THE ONLY RULE WE CAN FOLLOW IS THAT OUR ACTIONS MUST MOVE US TOWARD BECOMING LIKE GOD.**

NOW. AND NOW. AND NOW.

The greatest weapon we have in the war of transformation is this moment, because every second we live is an opportunity. **EVERY IRRITATION IS A CHANCE TO EMBRACE DISCOMFORT AND CHIP AWAY ANOTHER ATOM OF EGO. EVERY ENCOUNTER IS ONE MORE CHANCE TO CONFRONT SELFISHNESS AND SHARE WITH SOMEBODY.** This is the victory of triviality, because every moment is trivial, and it is in the trivial and humble that transformation is won. Grand gestures and dramatic moments don't last. What does is the now and the now and the now.

It is now that those who will complete the journey are separated from those who won't. It is now that we remember our nature and our goal. We are here to become like God and now we will not forget, nor will we forget that what is presented to us is exactly what we need to further our journey. **THERE IS NO "I WILL WAIT FOR THIS TO PASS SO I CAN GET BACK TO MY JOB OF BECOMING LIKE GOD." THERE IS NO DIVERSION. EVERY BEND AND FORK IN THE ROAD *IS* THE ROAD.**

Someone asks us for coffee, and we rush to oblige. But we do not forget why we're doing it. Not so he will like us, not so we will look spiritual, but because this act of sharing will awaken our divine nature. The more we remember, the more we remain conscious, the more intense the transformation. Someone cuts in front of us in line. We want to react with anger. We don't, because we know that restricting ourselves will break down one more barrier between us and God.

In this way we come to understand the truth about sacrifice. We call it sacrifice because we believe we're giving up something of value. But through sacrifice, all we're giving up are the toxic thoughts and actions of our Desire to Receive for the Self Alone.

Do it in this moment and that moment and the next. Do it with a stubbed toe and a cold cup of coffee and someone breaking into line.

Your life depends on it.

HATE EGO. SHARE RIDICULOUSLY NOW. AND NOW. AND NOW.

CHAPTER ELEVEN:
THE ZOHAR

The Baal Shem Tov was one of the rare giants of history who completed his own journey to becoming like God. When a negative decree would come down, and evil was descending on his people, the Baal Shem Tov would go to a particular place in the forest, light a fire, and say a special prayer. Then, a miracle would occur and the misfortune would be removed.

A generation later, when his disciple the Magid of Mezritch had to intervene with the heavens, he would go to the same place in the forest and say, "Master of the universe, hear me. I don't now how to pray like my master, but still I light the fire."

And the miracle was performed yet again.

In the following generation, when the Magid's disciple, Rav Moses Lev had to intervene with the heavens, he also went into the forest and said, "I don't know how to light the fire, I don't know the prayer, but I remember the place, and I believe that is enough."

And it was enough.

In the following generation, the student put his head in his hands and addressed God: "Master of the universe, hear me. I no longer know how to light the fire, I don't know the prayer, I can't even find the place in the forest. All I know is how to tell the story, and I believe that is enough."

And it was enough.

To merely pick up the Zohar, the Book of Splendor, to simply scan its Aramaic letters and allow in the energy that infuses them, is to come face to face with what Kabbalists have seen for thousands of years as the most powerful of all tools for annihilating the ego and reuniting with God.

It's a force of energy embedded in the pages of a book.

WE CONNECT TO THE ZOHAR TO BECOME LIKE GOD.

It's the central text, tool, and technology of Kabbalah.

It's the source of the secrets to becoming like God.

The Zohar defies definition. It's a vast and comprehensive guidebook to the lost godly nature of our souls. It's a compendium of virtually all information pertaining to the universe, whose wisdom science is only beginning to verify today. But its codes, its metaphors, and its cryptic language are not given to us purely for understanding. They also serve as channels for energy, whether we understand them or not. The Zohar not only expresses the energy of God, it embodies the energy of God.

FROM THE TIME OF THE CREATION OF THIS WORLD, KNOWING THE JOB WE WOULD FACE OF TRANSFORMING AND BECOMING LIKE GOD, THE CREATOR PREPARED A PLACE WHERE THE WISDOM FOR THIS TRANSFOR-MATION, AND THE POWER AND ENERGY FOR COMPLETING IT, WOULD BE STORED. SO WE CONNECT TO THE ZOHAR TO BECOME LIKE GOD. And when we're reading it, studying it, or scanning it, we're letting the energy of creation that lives in the shapes of those Aramaic letters speak, silently and mysteriously in the language of another world, directly to our souls

THE DOMAIN OF GIANTS

They're a lineage of giants, men and women who completed themselves, overcame the Opponent, and became like God. Along the way they left portals for the rest of us so that we, too, plug into their power.

It's no coincidence that all these great souls gathered together to reveal the Light of the Zohar. Rav Shimon bar Yochai revealed the totality of the Zohar 2,000 years ago, in collaboration with a historical assemblage of transformed beings—some in body, some in soul— an assemblage that included no less than Moses and Elijah. Thereafter, the giants who followed drew their wisdom and energy from that single power source and formed the wisdom of Kabbalah from its revelations.

A book that a transformed being bestows on generations to come is not merely information, or a record of a life, or a compendium of ideas. It is a mobile power unit, a direct transmission of energy encased within a spiritual battery. It remains accessible forever after to all of us who need to harness their power for the battle we wage.

To connect in this way with the energy of giants is an act of conscious intention. We pick up the Zohar, if not in fear and trembling, at least in awe and respect. We're in the presence of a force field. When a Kabbalist writes, his essence is injected into the work. **WE WANT TO CONNECT TO HIS CONSCIOUSNESS,**

WE CONNECT TO THE ZOHAR TO BECOME LIKE GOD.

HIS POWER, HIS CERTAINTY, HIS CLARITY, SO
WE CAN AWAKEN OUR OWN LIMITED CON-
SCIOUSNESS. OUR READING OF THE ZOHAR
CONNECTS US DIRECTLY TO THE CONSCIOUS-
NESS OF RAV SHIMON BAR YOCHAI.

*One day, as Rav Shimon bar Yochai went
out with his son, they saw the world plunge
suddenly into darkness. All light was gone
from the world, and an angel appeared, the
size of a huge mountain, blowing thirty
flames of fire from his mouth.*

*Rav Shimon spoke: "What do you intend
to do?"*

*The angel answered, "I am going to destroy
the world, since there are not thirty righteous men in this generation."*

*Rav Shimon said to him, "Go, if you
please, before the Holy One and say to
Him, "If there are not thirty righteous men
in the world, there are twenty, and if there
are not twenty, then there are ten, for it is
written that the world will not be destroyed
for the ten's sake. If there are not ten, there
are two—my son and I—for it is decreed
that two are sufficient. If there be not two,
there is one—I, Rav Shimon—for it is*

written that one righteous person is an ever-lasting foundation."

A voice resounded from heaven at that moment, saying, "Happy is your portion, Rav Shimon. The Holy One issues a decree, and yet you annul it down below.

This is the lesson of the angel of destruction: **WHEN WE ARE FULLY CONNECTED TO GOD, AS WAS RAV SHIMON, WHEN WE HAVE TRIUMPHED OVER EGO AND FULLY CONNECTED TO OUR GODLY NATURE, THEN WE CAN STOP ALL HARM—EVEN THE DESTRUCTION OF THE WORLD.**

Rav Moses Luzzatto was another giant. He saw the world as a great maze where human beings wander in ignorance while the souls of the transformed, those who overcame the Opponent, sit on tree limbs above and direct us.

The maze we wander today is a six-billion-people-strong collective consciousness of pain, suffering, and death, a six-billion-people-strong belief in the ultimate value of ego. We are each a part of that world consciousness, each of us dominated by awesome forces mobilized on the side of ego and Darkness. The journey to God has no hope of completion without a massive infusion of Light energy, courtesy of the giants

WE CONNECT TO THE ZOHAR TO BECOME LIKE GOD.

sitting up there on their tree limbs. Their consciousness is more important than their wisdom. Their energy
arms us against the inertia of six billion.

Rav Shimon bar Yochai, in essence, lives in dimensions
deep inside the atoms of the letters of the Zohar, available online, a power source free of the limits of this
world. Batteries are always included.

THE ROCK LONGS TO RETURN TO THE MOUNTAIN

It begins with the mountain. It ends with the mountain.

In between, there is the age of rocks.

Rocks are pieces of mountain, identical in essence,
existing only by virtue of separation.

Human beings are pieces of God, identical in essence,
existing only by virtue of separation.

Like rocks longing to merge again with the mountain,
humans long to return to God, but in the case of humans,
God also yearns for us to return to Him, with an even
greater yearning than our own, and offers His assistance.

> *A student of Rav Ashlag approached him
> sadly. "Master, I have tried to get rid of the*

Darkness within me. I have tried to break the Desire to Receive for the Self Alone. I have worked on diminishing my ego. I have done everything you taught. But I have to admit something." The student paused, apprehensively. "I have to tell you that, though I have tried everything in my power, I cannot do it." He dropped his head.

To the student's shock, Rav Ashlag clapped his hands with joy. "But master," the student said, "I know how much I disappoint you by my failure to understand your teachings. Why are you so happy?"

Rav Ashlag spoke. "You cannot achieve the transformation I've been teaching without the assistance of the Creator. And you cannot receive God's assistance unless you deeply understand that you're unable to change without it."

The journey of becoming like God may loom as an insurmountable task, but **IT'S OUR GREAT FORTUNE THAT WE'RE NOT ALONE. WE MERELY NEED THE CERTAINTY THAT ASSISTANCE IS REQUIRED. AND WHEN THAT CERTAINTY IS ACHIEVED, THE ASSISTANCE WILL COME.** As the great Kabbalist Rav Brandwein once wrote to my father, who was busy on the path of being the first

WE CONNECT TO THE ZOHAR TO BECOME LIKE GOD.

Kabbalist ever to spread the Zohar throughout the world: **"DO NOT WORRY, BECAUSE THERE ARE MORE FORCES ON OUR SIDE THAN ON THEIRS."**

There are more forces on our side than theirs.

He meant that we have the help of giants who have come before and on whose shoulders we stand. We have the help of a unique power source called the Zohar. And, of course, when our commitment is unyielding, we have the help of God.

CHAPTER TWELVE:

"THE OCEAN OF ALL THE TEARS OF ALL THE PEOPLE"

When a great master died, his son waited, certain that his father would soon appear to him in either a dream or a vision and report from the next world.

But his father never came.

When someone asked if the visit had finally occurred, the son replied that it hadn't. "However, I visited the heavenly court last night to ask the angels what had become of my father. 'He was here,' they replied, 'but he did not stay.'

"So I searched every region of heaven, inquiring of the angels if they had seen him,

and in each place they gave the same answer: 'Your father was here, but he continued walking.' Finally, I came upon a man sitting at the entrance to a forest and asked, 'Have you seen my father?' He too answered, 'Yes, he was here, but he continued walking.' Then he added, 'You will find him on the other side of the forest.'

"So I trekked through the forest, it seemed like days, and finally I reached a place where the trees ended. There, stretching as far as the eye could see, was a vast, heaving ocean with waves as tall as mountains. My father was standing there, staring into the turbulent waters.

"I approached him and took his arm. 'What are you doing here?' I asked. 'We were all worried. You did not return to us in a vision or a dream.'

"Without taking his eyes off the ocean, my father said: 'Do you know what this ocean is, my son?' I told him I did not. He said: 'This is the ocean of all the tears of all the people of the world who have ever cried from pain and suffering. I have sworn before God that I will never leave this ocean until He dries up all their tears.

BECOMING LIKE GOD IS THE ULTIMATE FORM OF COMPASSION.

Transformation is not a private enterprise.

You don't curl up in an easy chair and become like God.

THE JOURNEY TO GOD IS A LIBERATION OF A MINUSCULE CORNER OF THE UNIVERSE CALLED <u>YOUR NAME HERE</u>, TO UNIFICATION WITH LIVES EVERYWHERE, TO A COMPASSION THAT EXTENDS TO EVERY BEING IN EXISTENCE AND TO THE VAST OCEAN OF SUFFERING THAT ENGULFS THEM SIMPLY BECAUSE THEY WERE BORN INTO THIS WORLD.

The Desire to Receive for the Self Alone creates a divisive membrane of insensitivity. It allows us to focus on the amazing story of "me," oblivious to pain and death in others. **BECOMING LIKE GOD DEMANDS AN OBLITERATION OF THAT SEPARATION—IT DEMANDS THAT WE END FOR ETERNITY EVERY DISTINCTION, BORDER, AND BOUNDARY BETWEEN WHAT IS US AND WHAT IS NOT US.**

TO BE LIKE GOD IS TO NOT BE TWO WITH THE UNIVERSE. IT IS TO BE ONE.

Compassion for life everywhere is not just a matter of being nice, sympathetic, and generous. Compassion is what emerges from the ashes of Desire to Receive for the Self Alone, when, just as every being is God's business, every being becomes our business as well. "We experience our thoughts and feelings as something separated from the rest," Einstein once said. "It's a kind of optical delusion of consciousness."

In the Bible, Noah was saved during the flood with a male and female of every species, while the world around him was destroyed. He was, as we know, a righteous man. But the Bible also judges Noah a failure. He failed to fulfill his potential. How exactly does saving the world from extinction qualify as unfulfilled potential?

Noah lacked the ability to feel the pain of others. He neither prayed nor cried out as his fellow humans died in a global apocalypse. Today, modern apocalypses still occur on this butchered earth where microchips perform millions of operations per second but still can't eradicate starvation, disease, and the flare-ups of human cruelty known as the nightly news. **THERE CAN BE NO SPIRITUAL GROWTH WITHOUT A COMPASSION THAT DOESN'T FORGET, AND DRIVES US UNTIL EVERY BEING IS LIBERATED.**

In Kabbalah, compassion is not a sentimental notion. It is a force of the universe, like the laws of physics. "Looking out for Number One" is not wrong because it isn't nice. It's wrong because it violates the laws of physics, the connectedness scientists have called the Unified Field. Hundreds of years ago, the great Kabbalist known as the Baal Shem Tov taught there are no coincidences in this universe. Everything exists for a purpose. Simply because by coming to our attention, even negative events are somehow influenced by us. By a logic as yet unfathomable, when we witness a tragedy, in some way we are responsible for it.

This means **THERE ARE NO INNOCENT BYSTANDERS IN THE COLLISION KNOWN AS LIFE, NO VIEWING STAND FROM WHICH TO ENJOY THE FESTIVITIES. WITH TRANSFOR-MATION COMES RESPONSIBILITY.** My father being a great scholar and Kabbalist, I grew up amid stories of the great spiritual heroes, and I was particularly struck by the example of Moses. He abandoned a life of comfort in the house of Pharaoh and endured the pain and suffering of leading the Israelites from slavery. His compassion for human misery vastly outweighed his attachment to comfort. I used to think men like Moses were there to admire, but I subsequently found out they were there to emulate. The time comes for each of us to leave Pharaoh's boudoir and venture from a comfortable mediocrity. To let indignation grow and compassion flourish, on behalf of both those in the nightmare wings of the prison, "the wretched of the earth" and those in the white collar wing, the ones who can afford cable TV but are equally separated from God, equally sentenced to die.

A man once made the long journey to his teacher to bring him sad news: The man had a son whose medical condition had become grave and doctors had given up hope. Without his teacher's intercession, the son would surely die. "Is there anything you can do to help?"

The master began to pray and meditate, trying everything in his power, but after hours of effort, he turned sadly to his student. "I'm sorry," he said, "but the gates of heaven are closed. There is nothing I can do for your son."

The man was desolate. He got on his horse and began traveling home. As evening fell, he heard a horse galloping behind him. He turned around and saw his master.

Immediately, he thought perhaps the master had been able to open up the gates of heaven after all. "What's the news?" he asked eagerly. "I'm sorry," said the master. "The gates of heaven are still closed. But after you left, I realized that even if I cannot help you with my prayers and meditations, at least I can cry with you. That is why I have come." The two men sat together on a rock by the side of the road and wept.

BECOMING LIKE GOD IS THE ULTIMATE FORM OF COMPASSION.

Compassion is the mandate to feel. To do what we can. To share, to help, to lessen whatever suffering is in our power to alleviate. Or, to just sit with another on a rock and weep. **BUT THE MOST POWERFUL FORM OF COMPASSION IS TO DRAW MORE LIGHT INTO THE WORLD. TO LET THE PAIN AND SUFFERING FUEL OUR JOURNEY TO BECOMING LIKE GOD, AND HELP OTHERS ON THEIR JOURNEY SO THAT INSTEAD OF CHIPPING AWAY AT THE EARTH'S PAIN, WE CREATE A FORCE OF TRANSFORMED BEINGS OF UNIMAGINABLE POWER. IN THE MANDATE TO FREE THE WORLD FROM SUFFERING, BECOMING LIKE GOD BECOMES THE ULTIMATE ACT OF COMPASSION.**

"Do not go gentle into that good night," wrote Welsh poet Dylan Thomas. "Rage, rage against the dying of the light." For all his eloquence, Thomas was slightly mistaken, because the Light never dies. It is only we, born into to a prison as we are, who don't see it.

With unending compassion, we rage against the dying of the light. But not when we die.

We rage against the dying of the light when we're alive.

A WINDOW IN
OUR HEARTS

A great Kabbalist once took his closest student to a window and sat there with him for hours. The two cried the whole time.

When the master had left, the other students rushed to the window. "What did our master show you?" they demanded to know.

The student replied, "He showed me all the Light that will be revealed—all the joy and all the fulfillment—when a critical mass of people have transformed . . . when we have done our work."

"That made you both cry?" the students asked in surprise.

The student answered, "Yes, because he also showed me all the pain and all the suffering the world will have to go through in order to reach that fulfillment."

Each night, when I put my children to bed, I feel gratitude for having encountered the wisdom I've shared with you here. As I feel the love for my children, I know this information can save them. Then I'm struck with fear: What if I do not complete it? What if the world does not complete the journey? What will become of my children, what will become of your children, if we don't walk through the door that has opened and become like God?

What if pain, suffering, and death triumph?

Then I remember, with utter certainty: It is our destiny to become like God.

Every one of us has a window in our hearts, a window that shows us what could be. Our job, whenever we come across somebody in pain, is to take him or her to that window and point out what is waiting for us on the other side of suffering.

OUR JOB IS TO HELP THE WORLD ACHIEVE A CRITICAL MASS OF PEOPLE ON THE PATH TO BECOMING LIKE GOD, SO THAT PAIN, SUFFERING, AND DEATH WILL VANISH. To so care

OUR DESTINEY IS TO BECOME LIKE GOD.

about the world is part of the process of becoming like God, because feeling mankind's pain, and striving ceaselessly for an end to it, is an aspect of being like God.

OUR DESTINY IS TO BECOME LIKE GOD.

The Opponent will try to make us forget. We will not forget. He will try to weaken our resolve to change. We will not let this happen. We will remind ourselves repeatedly of what we're trying to do and why we're trying to do it.

OUR DESTINY IS TO BECOME LIKE GOD.

We will open the gates of a prison, for ourselves, for our children, and for the world.

OUR DESTINY IS TO BECOME LIKE GOD.

And remove pain, suffering, and death, forever.

MORE FROM NATIONAL BEST SELLING AUTHOR MICHAEL BERG

THE SECRET

Like a jewel that has been painstakingly cut and polished, *The Secret* reveals life's essence in its most concise and powerful form. Michael Berg begins by showing you how our everyday understanding of our purpose in the world is literally backwards. Whenever there is pain in our lives—indeed, whenever there is anything less than complete joy and fulfillment—this basic misunderstanding is the reason.

As the book continues, you will be introduced to stories and insights from the greatest sages of Kabbalah. You will learn how you can free yourself from unhappiness and gain the joy and fulfillment that is your true destiny. *The Secret* is a book that will open your eyes, touch your heart, and change your life forever!

MORE PRODUCTS THAT CAN HELP YOU BRING THE WISDOM OF KABBALAH INTO YOUR LIFE

THE 72 NAMES OF GOD: TECHNOLOGY FOR THE SOUL™
—a national best-seller by author Yehuda Berg

The story of Moses and the Red Sea is well known to almost everyone; it's even been an Academy Award–winning film. What is not known, according to the internationally prominent Kabbalist Rabbi Yehuda Berg, is that a state-of-the-art technology is encoded and concealed within that biblical story. This technology is called the 72 Names of God, and it is the key—your key—to ridding yourself of depression, stress, creative stagnation, anger, illness, and other physical and emotional problems. In fact, the 72 Names of God is the oldest, most powerful tool known to mankind—far more powerful than any 21st century high-tech know-how when it comes to eliminating the garbage in your life so that you can wake up and enjoy life each day. Indeed, the 72 Names of God is the ultimate pill for anything and everything that ails you because it strikes at the DNA level of your soul.

THE POWER OF KABBALAH
—an international best-seller by author Yehuda Berg

Imagine your life filled with unending joy, purpose, and contentment. Imagine your days infused with pure insight and energy. This is *The Power of Kabbalah*. It is the path from the momentary pleasure that most of us settle for to the lasting fulfillment that is yours to claim. Your deepest desires are waiting to be realized. But they are not limited to the temporary rush you might get from closing a business deal, the short-term high from drugs, or a passionate sexual relationship that lasts for only a few short months.

Wouldn't you like to experience a lasting sense of wholeness and peace that is unshakable, no matter what might be happening around you? Complete fulfillment is the promise of Kabbalah. Within these pages, you will learn how to look at and navigate through life in a whole new way. You will understand your purpose and how to receive the abundant gifts that are waiting for you. By making a critical transformation from a reactive to a proactive being, you will increase your creative energy, gain control of your life, and enjoy new spiritual levels of existence. Kabbalah's ancient teaching is rooted in the perfect union of the physical and spiritual laws already at work in your life. Get ready to experience this exciting realm of awareness, meaning, and joy.

The wonder and wisdom of Kabbalah have influenced the world's leading spiritual, philosophical, religious, and scientific minds. Until today, however, that wisdom was hidden away in ancient texts, available only to scholars who knew where to look. Now, after many centuries, *The Power of Kabbalah* resides in this one remarkable book. Here at long last is the complete and simple path—actions you can take right now to create the life you desire and deserve.

THE ESSENTIAL ZOHAR
By Rav Berg

The Zohar has traditionally been known as the world's most esoteric and profound spiritual document, but Rav Berg has dedicated his life to making this wisdom universally available. The vast wisdom and Light of the Zohar came into being as a gift to all humanity, and *The Essential Zohar* at last explains this gift to the world.

AUDIO RESOURCES

THE POWER OF KABBALAH TAPE SERIES

The Power of Kabbalah is nothing less than a user's guide to the universe. Move beyond where you are right now to where you truly want to be—emotionally, spiritually, and creatively. This exciting tape series brings you the ancient, authentic teaching of Kabbalah in a powerful, practical audio format.

CREATING MIRACLES IN YOUR LIFE

We're used to thinking of a miracle as something that happens at the whim of God. But the Kabbalists have long taught that the true power to create miracles is present in each and every one of us—if only we can learn to access that power and put it into practice. This inspiring tape series shows how to do exactly that. Order it now, and enter the zone of the miraculous!

THE ZOHAR

"BRINGING THE ZOHAR FROM NEAR OBLIVION TO WIDE ACCESSIBILITY HAS TAKEN MANY DECADES. IT IS AN ACHIEVEMENT OF WHICH WE ARE TRULY PROUD AND GRATEFUL."

—Michael Berg

Composed more than 2,000 years ago, the Zohar is a set of 23 books, a commentary on biblical and spiritual matters in the form of conversations among spiritual masters. But to describe the Zohar only in physical terms is greatly misleading. In truth, the Zohar is nothing less than a powerful tool for achieving the most important purposes of our lives. It was given to all humankind by the Creator to bring us protection, to connect us with the Creator's Light, and ultimately to fulfill our birthright of true spiritual transformation.

Eighty years ago, when the Kabbalah Centre was founded, the Zohar had virtually disappeared from the world. Few people in the general population had ever heard of it. Whoever sought to read it—in any country, in any language, at any price—faced a long and futile search. Today all this has changed. Through the work of the Kabbalah Centre and the editorial efforts of Michael Berg, the Zohar is now being brought to the world, not only in the original Aramaic language but also in English.

The new English Zohar provides everything for connecting to this sacred text on all levels: the original Aramaic text for scanning; an English translation; and clear, concise commentary for study and learning.

THE KABBALAH CENTRE
THE INTERNATIONAL LEADER IN THE EDUCATION OF KABBALAH

Since its founding, the Kabbalah Centre has had a single mission: to improve and transform people's lives by bringing the power and wisdom of Kabbalah to all who wish to partake of it.

Through the lifelong efforts of Rav Berg, his wife Karen, and the great spiritual lineage of which they are a part, an astonishing 3.5 million people around the world have already been touched by the powerful teachings of Kabbalah. And each year, the numbers are growing!

As the leading source of Kabbalistic wisdom with 50 locations around the world, the Kabbalah Centre offers you a wealth of resources, including:

- The English Zohar, the first-ever comprehensive English translation of the foundation of Kabbalistic wisdom. In 23 beautifully bound volumes, this edition includes the full Aramaic text, the English translation, and detailed commentary, making this once-inaccessible text understandable to all.

- A full schedule of workshops, lectures, and evening classes for students at all levels of knowledge and experience.

- CDs, audiotapes and videotapes, and books in English and ten other languages.

- One of the Internet's most exciting and comprehensive websites, **www.kabbalah.com**—which receives more than 100,000 visitors each month.

- A constantly expanding list of events and publications to help you live *The Secret* and other teachings of Kabbalah with greater understanding and excitement.

Discover why the Kabbalah Centre is one of the world's fastest-growing spiritual organizations. Our sole purpose is to improve people's lives through the teachings of Kabbalah. Let us show you what Kabbalah can do for you!

Each Kabbalah Centre location hosts free introductory lectures. For more information on Kabbalah or on these and other products and services, call 1-800-KABBALAH.

Wherever you are, there's a Kabbalah Centre—because now you can call 1-800-KABBALAH from almost anywhere, 18 hours a day, and get answers or guidance right over the telephone. You'll be connected to distinguished senior faculty who are on hand to help you understand Kabbalah as deeply as you want to— whether it involves recommending a course of study; deciding which books/tapes to take or the order in which to take them; discussing the material; or anything else you wish to know about Kabbalah.

IF YOU HAVE ANY QUESTIONS FOR MICHAEL,
WOULD LIKE TO LEARN MORE, SHARE MORE,
AND BE PART OF A COMMUNITY OF PEOPLE
ON THE JOURNEY TO BECOMING LIKE GOD,
PLEASE VISIT

WWW.BECOMINGLIKEGOD.COM

THERE, YOU'LL DISCOVER MORE LESSONS,
STORIES, AND TOOLS TO HELP YOU BECOME
LIKE GOD.